A HISTORY OF
THE PREBENDAL SCHOOL

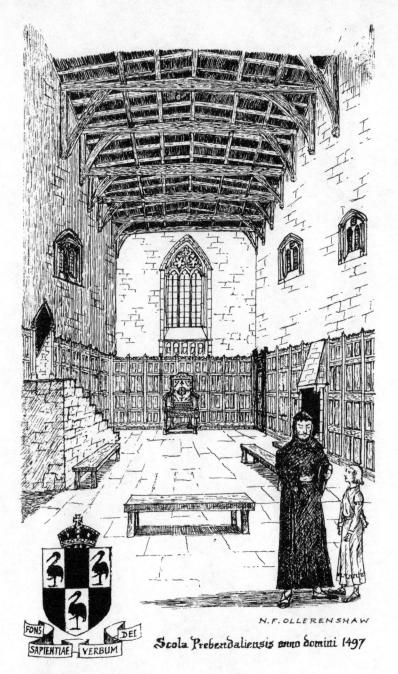

FONS SAPIENTIAE VERBUM DEI

N.F. OLLERENSHAW

Scola Prebendaliensis anno domini 1497

Frontispiece: A reconstruction of the old school-room as it might have appeared in 1497.

A History of
The Prebendal School

Neville Ollerenshaw

Phillimore

1984

Published by
PHILLIMORE & CO. LTD.
Shopwyke Hall, Chichester, Sussex

ISBN 0 85033 552 3

Printed and bound in Great Britain by
BILLING & SONS LTD
Worcester, England

DEDICATION

To my wife, Nony,

*for whom, as for myself, the shared years at the Prebendal
School will always remain the happiest of memories*

CONTENTS

LIST OF PLATES

(between pages 46 and 47)

Frontispiece: A reconstruction of the old school-room

PICTORIAL ACKNOWLEDGMENTS

The photograph used for plate no. 1 was taken by my former colleague Mr. David Smith. Nos. 4, 5 and 7 are reproduced by courtesy of *The Times* newspaper and nos. 9 and 10 by courtesy of Portsmouth and Sunderland Newspapers Ltd.

FOREWORD

This is clearly a work of love, but it is also the outcome of patient and detailed research, bringing the history of our school up to date. It is published at a time when a new chapter in the government of the Prebendal is about to open with the establishment, under revised Cathedral statutes, of a governing body which will include members additional to The Dean and Administrative Chapter.

This is a story told by one who knows the school from inside and really understands its history and present ethos. We are greatly indebted to Mr. Ollerenshaw for his work, which needs but one addition—which is a very grateful acknowledgement of the special contribution to the Prebendal of Neville and his wife, Nony, whom Prebendalians and many others remember with respect, admiration and affection.

ROBERT HOLTBY,
Dean; Chairman of the Governors

August, 1984

INTRODUCTION

THE FIRST TIME that I set foot in Chichester Cathedral was in the summer of 1935 when as a chorister from Winchester I took part in one of the pre-war festivals. My family had seats in the chancel, and the Winchester boys were placed in the front stalls beneath the organ loft. Though I still retain a boy's eye-view of the occasion, I cannot help reflecting how incredulous I would have been, had it been revealed to me then that thirty-four years later I should be occupying as Headmaster of the Prebendal School the stall directly behind where I sang that day.

Returning in 1969, I never experienced the expected conflict of loyalties, for Chichester exerts such a charm that I quickly became enthralled, and nearly fourteen years spent in the shadow of the cathedral were enough to convert me into an ardent Cicestrian. At the same time, as an historian at heart and by training, I was always profoundly conscious of belonging to a school whose origins could be traced back to the Middle Ages, of being heir to traditions that were almost timeless. Though pride may be one of the seven deadly sins, I am proud to have been associated with such a place.

When the Very Reverend Robert Holtby was installed as Dean in 1977, it soon became clear that we had two very important things in common, which were a lifelong interest in education and a strong commitment to the values and traditions of cathedral schools and to the continuing success of the Prebendal School in particular. So I could not have been more delighted when, as I approached retirement, he invited me to try my hand at producing a history of the school that would update and enlarge upon the booklet composed by Dorothy Howell-Thomas around 1935. This was a task after my own heart and has helped to cushion me against the shock of having too much leisure after years of having too little.

If the resultant book appears insubstantial in the light of the centuries that the school has been in being, it is due in great measure to a lamentable scarcity of records. Who knows what documents were burned when Sir Arthur Hazelrigge turned a blind eye to the depredations of Waller's troopers and the cathedral library was sacked? And how much evidence from later times was recycled to meet the demand for paper in two World Wars?

In the absence of other sources I have had perforce to rely quite heavily upon articles contained on Volumes 2 and 3 of the *Victoria History of the County of Sussex*, and for my background material I am indebted to A. F. Leach's *Schools of Medieval England*, and to Nicholas Orme's *English Schools in the Middle Ages*.

In chronicling more recent events I would like to acknowledge with gratitude the invaluable help that I have received from the late Mrs. Eve Powell and from the Rev. Peter Head, the Rev. A. R. Duncan-Jones, Mr. Ralph Elliott, Mr. Guy Hepburn, the Rev. Bernard Bate and Mrs. Bate, Mr. Roger Heath-Bullock, and Mr. Keith Ross, all of whom so patiently answered my questions and took the greatest pains to set down their recollections in writing.

The books ends in 1982 because that was as far as my brief ran, but a school is a living organism and another chapter is already in the making. No doubt with the passage of time another hand will take up the story from where I have left it. In the meantime I am sure that under the leadership of my successor, the Rev. Godfrey Hall, the school will continue to prosper and 'all good learning flourish and abound'.

Beccles, Suffolk   N.F.O.

Chapter One

ORIGINS AND EARLY HISTORY: THE MIDDLE AGES

THE PREBENDAL SCHOOL is so called because in 1497 Bishop Story converted a canonry—the Prebend of High-leigh—into an endowment for his new grammar school, but in so doing he was only restructuring and giving a new lease of life to a foundation that already existed. Indeed it is possible that the flint building on West Street that it occupied had been in continuous use as a school since it was first erected in the thirteenth century—an event that may well have coincided with the issue of Statutes in 1232—but on the other hand it has been argued that it could previously have been the hall of one of the canons' residences, and Ian Nairn (co-author with Nikolaus Pevsner of the volume on Sussex in the *Buildings of England* series) evidently supports this theory.

Even so there are reasonable grounds for the claim that the school, however named, is the oldest in Sussex; indeed, it is more than probable that its history is, in fact, as long as that of the cathedral that it served, for there is ample evidence that in Norman times, perhaps even earlier, a school formed an integral part of the foundation of a cathedral. So it is quite possible that when, by decree of the Synod of London in 1075, the see established by Saint Wilfrid was moved from Selsey to Chichester, either an existing school moved with it or one was created along with the new cathedral.

In the absence of documentary records it would be idle to speculate on the location of such a school within the cathedral precinct, but by referring to those of other secular cathedrals one may form some conclusions as to its nature and organisation.

1

At the outset the school must have been what was termed a 'Song School', housing and teaching the cathedral choristers. The title still attaches to the Chapter House above the Canons' Vestry, where the choir normally holds its practices, but in medieval times it embraced all schools that in modern terminology would be called primaries, and referred to the institutions themselves. They, of course, taught reading and elementary grammar and they were open to boys from the locality, but the presence of choristers and others who served in the church led to an emphasis on the teaching of plainsong, which so dominated the curriculum that the term —'Song School'— became in common parlance the most apt description of them.

The children who attended Song Schools were probably aged between seven and ten and they came in daily for their lessons, but the choristers, who were often chosen from among those enrolled, were commonly housed and fed by the cathedral authorities. Unlike other scholars, they received free board and lodging and free schooling in return for their services in the choir. At most cathedrals in the later Middle Ages there were between 10 and 14 of them, and they were taught song by the Precentor or his deputy, the Succentor, but then, as is to a lesser extent the case today, it was difficult to give the choristers a good general education because their attendance at practices and services claimed so much of their time.

At a fairly early date it seems that the Song School of Chichester Cathedral was extended to include older boys in and about the city and duly became known as a Grammar School. In such a school the traditional subjects studied were Latin, Grammar, Rhetoric and Logic, and originally it was the Chancellor of the cathedral who was responsible for the teaching, but from the thirteenth century onwards it was normal practice for him to appoint a schoolmaster to act as his deputy, leaving him free to concentrate on his other duties, which included lecturing to the local clergy on theology and canon law. The Statutes of 1232 show that this was the case in Chichester and, as at other secular cathedrals, the master was usually a cleric, who as such was entitled to a seat in the stalls and might augment his salary by serving one of the cathedral chantries or by acting as a vicar-choral.

Although song and grammar were successive stages in a boy's education, it did not necessarily follow that they were taught in different institutions, and it is clear that in Chichester scholars at both levels studied under the same roof.

The thirteenth-century schoolhouse on West Street started life as a single lofty room with a vaulted cellar beneath it. Originally the pitch of the roof must have been somewhat steeper and in winter the draughty schoolroom would have been heated by an open fire set in the west wall. The room was certainly long enough to enable children of different ages and levels to be taught simultaneously at opposite ends of it. The arrangement would have been similar to that of Manchester Grammar School, where scholars were appointed by the master on a monthly rota to teach the alphabet to the juniors who sat at one end of the room, while grammarians were taught at the other. Since this system was adopted by Robert Sherborne, Bishop of Chichester, when he founded Rolleston Grammar School in Staffordshire in 1524, it is highly probable that he borrowed the idea from the school that stood cheek by jowl with his palace.

During the fifteenth century the standard charge for fee-paying pupils was about eight pence a quarter, and a master would need large classes to ensure even a relatively modest income for himself, but he would often supplement his earnings by taking in boarders who might pay as much as a shilling a week for their keep. Insofar as people who set some store by a good education were prepared to send their children away to school, times have not changed, and in the Middle Ages it was recognised that better teaching was to be found in the university towns and the cathedral cities.

One would like to know more of these pre-Reformation masters and of the scholars who sat at their feet, but, because at Chichester so few records survive, one must perforce be content with but a few tantalising glimpses. Thus in 1384 we learn that John Bishopston, Chancellor of the cathedral, bequeathed his 'green robe with taffity covered with moons' to Master Thomas Romsey, rector of the Grammar School

of Chichester. Romsey was in 1394 appointed Headmaster
of Winchester College, being only the second to hold this
office, for William of Wykeham's foundation did not receive
its charter until 1382. He remained there on and off for
twenty-four years, and Winchester was later to return the
compliment by sending on masters to Chichester, which happened on several occasions before the Reformation and after.

During the fifteenth century the school would appear to
have suffered various misfortunes. Bishop Robert Reade,
conducting a visitation in 1402, complained that 'the Chancellor does not find a master diligent in teaching the choristers
grammar' and some sixty years later it is disclosed that the
headmaster, Thomas Gyldesburgh, who was also parson of
St Olave's in Chichester, was in prison for debt. Petitioning
in Chancery for his release, he declared that he had been a
schoolmaster for more than thirty years and was over eighty,
'right corpulent, and hath a malady in his leg that he may
neither well ride nor go'.

Another indication that the school had fallen on hard
times was that in an inflationary period its endowment does
not appear to have exceeded £2 13s. 4d. a year, a sum
which might have seemed generous when it was first allocated
as far back, perhaps, as the twelfth century. Edward Story,
when he became Bishop in 1478, spoke in scathing tones not
only about the ignorance of the Chichester clergy, but also
about the neglect of sound learning within the community.
He accordingly determined to reorganise the existing grammar
school, for which fresh Statutes were prepared. Thus it was
that in 1497 the Prebendal School came into being.

Chapter Two

THE NEW FOUNDATION: 1497

IT WAS DURING the fifteenth century that the great move-
ment began by which private benefactors from kings to
commoners founded endowed schools, and Bishop Story was
following an established precedent when he decided to devote
to his school moneys that had not hitherto been assigned to
education, but, whereas it was quite common to attach a
chantry to a school by way of endowment, the unusual
feature of Story's foundation was that he converted a
canonry for the purpose.

Among the thirty canons who from earliest times made up
the cathedral establishment there had been since at least the
end of the twelfth century a Prebendary of Highleigh and it
was with the consent of the then Prebendary, Nicholas
Taverner, who duly resigned his canonry, that the Bishop in
1497 attached the mastership of the Grammar School 'with
the burden of teaching' to the Prebend, so that all future
holders of the office would receive their stipend in virtue of
their service to the school. He gave no endowment to the
school itself either in land or in money. Besides drawing up
Statutes for the government of the school all the Bishop did
was to purchase from the Dean and Chapter the premises
in West Street in which the Prebendary was to live and
carry on the Grammar School. These are described as 'the
tenement called Furley, alias Ladynporch' and stood to the
west of the tenement of the Sub-Dean.

In his Statutes the Bishop, after a lengthy preamble in
which he bemoans the scarcity of good priests and extols
the benefits of grammar to character, goes on to define the
procedure by which future prebendaries are to be appointed,

5

their duties and the terms of their employment. He decrees that in summertime the 'Grammatici' and others attending the school on weekdays will start work at five o'clock or soon after, in winter before six o'clock, and that, when the bell rings for the morrow mass in St George's chapel, all must go to the cathedral, where, if they do not attend the whole service, they will at least be present for the elevation of the Host and thereafter return quietly and orderly to the Grammar School.

Back in school, the scholars, led by the Prebendary, had to sing or recite various prayers, psalms and responses, and other anthems and orisons were stipulated when they departed at nightfall. The Bishop also directed that a mass should be said for his soul every Friday, except Good Friday and Christmas Day, and that all the scholars should observe the anniversary of his death by attending the appointed requiem mass.

Like most of the endowed schools that were founded in this period, the Prebendal School now became a free grammar school. Indeed the Bishop expressly stipulated that 'the canon and prebendary . . . shall diligently, sufficiently, well and eloquently, freely and gratis teach, instruct, inform and chastise grammarians and others whomsoever coming to our school for the sake of learning, on no account by reason thereof or in any other way taking from the scholars or their parents or friends any sum of money or accepting gifts or other offerings, except thanks given and bestowed on him'.

It was also the Prebendary's responsibility to keep the building in repair and in this connection he was instructed that he should on no account let or grant free use of any part of the premises 'to laymen or secular persons, except the great cellar if that can be done without scandal or inconvenience to the scholars of our grammar school'.

The school that was thus reconstituted in 1497 consisted of the original thirteenth-century building, which was at that time some twenty feet short of its present length at its southern end, and the adjoining house, which was occupied by the master and is now number 53 West Street. The master's house did not at that time communicate with the school; nor was it linked with the building to the east of it, which was the residence of the Sub-Dean and was not added to the school until this century. The house was rebuilt by Dr. David Davis, who was Prebendary of Highleigh from 1784 to 1797, but traces of the earlier edifice came to light when the present school kitchen was stripped and reconstructed in 1979, uncovering Tudor brickwork and half-timbering on three sides of the room. Other remains of the original structure can be seen in the shape of a stone fireplace intriguingly located inside a broom cupboard on the first floor.

Bishop Story's Statutes included the proviso that the master of the grammar school should hold no benefice other than the prebend of Highleigh, but since the school prospered and this restriction must have seemed unduly harsh to a pluralistic generation of clergy, the Bishop made use of the power of amendment that he reserved to himself during his lifetime and in 1502 allowed the schoolmaster-prebendary to hold one other ecclesiastical benefice on condition that he appointed and paid an usher to assist in the teaching and maintenance of discipline 'for the benefit of the scholars flocking to the said school'.

In the light of the wording of the Statutes made by Bishop Story it has been argued that none of the amendments by later bishops, such as those of Bishop Day (1550), Bishop Carr (1828) and Bishop Durnford (1880), had any validity. As A. F. Leach expressed it, nothing but an overriding power derived from an Act of Parliament could do it, but such a contention comes too late to put the clock back. At all events, when the Chapter nominated John Wykley, B.A., as the first schoolmaster, and confirmation of his appointment was incorporated in the Statutes of 1497, the school entered a new era that was to last for more than four hundred years.

Chapter Three

BEAKS AND BOYS: 1497–1797

WYKLEY HELD OFFICE for little more than two years, being succeeded in 1500 by John Holt, B.A., a native of Sussex, who was a fellow of Magdalen College, Oxford, and had taught at Magdalen College School and in Archbishop Morton's household at Lambeth. He was a friend of Thomas More and a scholar of some distinction, who composed the first Latin grammar in English, which was published in 1500 by Wynkyn de Worde under the title of *Lac Puerorum* or *Mylke for Chyldren.*

Holt's time at the Prebendal School was as brief as that of his predecessor, for in 1502 he was appointed by King Henry VII to succeed the poet, John Skelton, as tutor to the eleven-year-old Prince of Wales, the future Henry VIII, who in that year had become heir to the throne.

Unfortunately for Chichester, the school was to retain its third master no longer than its first two, because William Hone, M.A., having taken Holt's place in 1502, was to follow him to the royal court when Holt died prematurely in 1504. He tutored the young Henry for four or five years, and subsequently became schoolmaster to Henry's sister, Mary.

It says much for the quality of these early headmasters that two in succession should have been chosen to teach England's future king and that Henry proved perhaps more learned and more versatile in his attainments than any of his predecessors. That the school succeeded in attracting such men suggests that the establishment was held in high esteem, and this is borne out by the appointment in 1504 of Nicholas Bradbrigge, M.A., who had formerly been Headmaster of Eton College. A further indication of its standing was given

8

when in 1531 John Tychenor, M.A., resigned the Headmastership of Winchester College to become headmaster of Chichester Grammar School, as it was sometimes termed.

Tychenor is credited with having produced while at Winchester a timetable that is almost unique in dating back to
pre-Reformation times, but the 'use' of Winchester, as it
was called, was in essence a collection of syllabuses for the
various forms in a public or grammar school. It was certainly
adopted by the newly-founded Saffron Walden School in
Essex and was probably introduced at Chichester as well.

In 1538 Tychenor gave up the school and exchanged the
prebend of Highleigh for that of Wittering, to which a theological lectureship was attached. He was succeeded by
Anthony Clarke, B.D., a Cistercian monk who, following
the dissolution of the monasteries, had become a secular
priest. It was when Clarke retired in 1550 that the bishop,
George Day, amended Story's Statutes to enable Thomas
Garbard, M.A., to be appointed, for the latter was not a
priest as stipulated in the earlier constitution. He was, in
fact, the only lay prebendary to be headmaster during the
entire span of the school's lifetime, for, although there have
been lay headmasters since, none has held the prebend to
which the headmastership was initially attached.

The most distinguished headmaster to hold office during
the second half of the sixteenth century was undoubtedly
Hugh Barker, another Wykehamist and a fellow of New
College, Oxford, who, in addition to his M.A. degree, was
a Bachelor or Civil Law and later obtained his doctorate in
that field, going on to become Chancellor of the Oxford
diocese and Dean of the Arches. Coming to Chichester in
1594, he was contemporary with the organist, Thomas
Weelkes, and probably taught both William Juxon, later
to become Archbishop of Canterbury, and John Selden, the
celebrated jurist.

Juxon, though born and brought up in Chichester, where
his father was the bishop's receiver, could only have acquired
his early education here, for in due course his family returned
to London and sent him to Merchant Taylors' School. He
was Lord High Treasurer to King Charles I, and as Bishop

of London attended the King on the scaffold when he met his death in 1649. Ironically one of the regicides whose name appears on the death warrant was another old Prebendalian, William Cawley. The son of a rich brewer of Chichester, Cawley at various times represented both Chichester and Midhurst in Parliament and is remembered locally as the founder of St Bartholomew's Hospital, part of which still stands. Excepted from the general amnesty that King Charles II proclaimed at his restoration in 1660, he fled first to the Low Countries, and then to Switzerland, where he died in 1667.

Selden, who, unlike Juxon, spent all his schooldays at the Prebendal School, must have derived his passion for the Law from Hugh Barker and from the latter's brother, Anthony, who was Principal of Hart Hall in Oxford, to which he went on from Chichester in 1600. Selden, whose legal utterances are preserved in a book called *Table Talk,* was four times elected to Parliament and was outspoken in his opposition to all forms of tyranny, which made him unpopular with both Church and King. In fact, at one stage it led to a spell of imprisonment. At his old school the boarders' common room is today named after him, and his portrait hangs over the mantelpiece.

The lives of these three men exemplify the extremes that were to divide the nation during the great Civil War, the impact of which was to be felt in Chichester quite soon after hostilities were first declared.

Times had been uneasy since 1616, when the Dean and Chapter ordered the 'precular' to clear the cathedral of 'hogs and dogs and lewd persons that play or do worse therein' and to 'admonish the schoolmasters concerning their scholars'. Indeed it was the absence of a proper playground that caused Archbishop Laud, in his visitation of 1634, to issue an injunction to the Dean and Chapter to 'use some means with Mr. Peter Coxe, an Alderman of the city of Chichester, that the piece of ground now in his possession be laid open again, that the scholars of your Free School may have liberty to play there as formerly they have had time out of mind'.

Excitement must have run high among the children of the Prebendal School when, in the days before Christmas 1642, the city shook to the bombardment of Sir William Waller's parliamentary artillery, and troops of the Royalist garrison were making ineffectual sorties through West Gate—only a hundred yards or so from the school entrance. Some may have·witnessed the invasion of the Cathedral by mounted Roundhead troopers which followed the surrender of the city on 29 December, and any choristers among them would have had cause to question their future as organ pipes were torn from their sockets and sheet music and psalters were consigned to the flames.

Although the Cathedral was severely damaged, the Dean and Chapter dismissed, and their members reduced to poverty, and although the Bishop himself was forced from his palace, which was subsequently sold to a Roundhead officer, Parliament took care to preserve cathedral grammar schools. So the Prebendal School survived, and its headmaster, George Collins, M.A., who had himself been a pupil at the school, and returned to take charge at the tender age of twenty-three, was voted an increase in his annual salary from twenty to thirty pounds. He supplanted George Elgar, LL.B., who receives a mention in Walker's *Sufferings of the Clergy,* but under the Commonwealth he was not a Prebendary of Highleigh.

The status quo was only restored with the return of King Charles II in 1660, when Collins moved on to Lewes Grammar School and was succeeded by Thomas Barter, B.A., the first of a new line of prebendaries that was to continue uninterrupted until the beginning of this century.

It was either in Barter's time or under his successor, John Baguley, M.A., that the Great Plague of 1665 struck Chichester, supposedly brought from London by a traveller who was carrying the infection and died at the inn where he was lodging. As others became infected and an epidemic developed, the City Council adopted the same measures as were in force in the capital. Houses in which cases of plague were reported were boarded up and cordoned off, but Chichester, being a walled city, was able to take the added precaution of shutting its gates to prevent people either coming in or going out. During that long sultry summer the school must have remained closed, as did churches and other places where citizens normally congregated. It was only with the arrival of a rainy autumn that the plague abated and the survivors were able to celebrate their deliverance with services of thanksgiving in all the city's churches. By the end of the year life was back to normal and the school once more in session.

Whereas there had been no fewer than twenty-five masters between 1497 and the end of the seventeenth century, the eighteenth century was remarkable in that the school was ruled by only six men, each of whom enjoyed a long term of office. This century also witnessed the foundation in 1702 of the Bluecoat School established under the will of Oliver Whitby, son of the Archdeacon of Chichester, and a former pupil of the Prebendal School. Whitby's Free School, as it came to be called, occupied a building on the opposite side of West Street and was designed to accommodate twelve Church of England scholars from the city or the neighbouring parishes of Harting and West Wittering.

Contrary to the popular tradition it was probably here rather than at the Prebendal School that William Collins, the poet, who was the son of a local hatter, began his education before going on by way of Winchester College to Oxford in 1741. There can be no doubt, however, that another poet, the Reverend James Hurdis, was at the Prebendal School between 1771 and 1780, for the connection was unexpectedly revived in 1946. In that year the great-granddaughter of the poet, Mrs. Mary Pearson of Guthrie in Scotland, presented the school with a small organ that he built for his room's at Magdalen College, Oxford. (The organ has been lodged for safe keeping in the Cathedral.)

Whitby's Free School was not the only rival establishment that came into being in the course of the eighteenth century, for William Clowes, the printer, noted that his father, an Oxford man, had kept a large school in Chichester, and that his mother, after she was widowed, ran a small private school. It is also on record that Hayley, the poet, received his early education in a school kept by three sisters called Russell, but, in spite of all these mushroom growths on the educational scene, the Prebendal School was still flourishing when the nineteenth century dawned.

Chapter Four

THE NINETEENTH CENTURY: SEE-SAW YEARS

ALTHOUGH AT THE TURN of the century the school seems to have been in good heart, by 1818 there were only forty boys, boarders and day-pupils included, the former paying sixty guineas, the latter eight guineas a year in fees. By this time the yield from the endowment was small since the lands of the prebend were let at the old rent of little more than £13 a year, the leases extending over three lives. Considerable premiums could be collected when leases fell due for renewal, but, as George Bliss, who was Headmaster at the time, complained, it was many years since any such renewal had taken place.

With the appointment of Charles Webber, M.A., in 1824, the fortunes of the school revived, partly perhaps because Bishop Carr in 1828 made new statutes restricting the number of free scholars to 'ten children born of Protestant parents resident in Chichester, or children of clergymen having cure of souls in the diocese', but also in large measure because it became the fashionable place for children to be educated. The Duke of Richmond and his brother, Lord Henry Lennox, used it as a preparatory school for Westminster, and it was patronised equally by the gentry of both county and city. As a result numbers swelled to between seventy and eighty boys, including some thirty or forty boarders.

Thus in 1830 sufficient funds were available for alterations to the school buildings. In this context Prebendary Webber was nothing if not thorough. The old school building was completely gutted, the turret vaulting of the great cellar removed and the roof raised to allow three storeys to be

14

made where there was previously only one. To provide adequate lighting new windows were let into the old flint walls at all levels, effectively destroying the original character of the building. The north end of the school where it over-looked West Street was completely rebuilt, and this section was divided from the main body of the building by a brick wall that extends from the basement to the roof. At the same time doorways were inserted in the eastern wall to connect the school with the master's house, and the passage which originally separated them was enclosed, making it a part of the house.

The top floor of the reconstructed building now became the schoolroom, incorporating the oak panelling that had originally lined the walls at the lower level; the floor below it was used as a dormitory; and the floor immediately above the basement acted as a washing room. These arrangements were completely altered by Webber's successor, the Reverend Thomas Brown, M.A., who soon after his appointment in 1840 abandoned the top storey entirely and turned the washing room into a schoolroom, which in part it still remains.

We are not told what provision was made for the boys to wash, but there is ample evidence that from this time the school went into a prolonged decline. By 1854 there were only eighteen boys, and six years later the school was the subject of complaint in the House of Commons, the members of which were told that the free scholars received free tuition in Greek and Latin only; for every other subject they were charged fees of £10 a year. There were still only eighteen boys in 1866, but by this date they were all under fourteen years of age so that the school already, albeit unintention-ally, had been transformed into a preparatory school.

This state of affairs appears to have continued until 1879, when, following the death of Mr. Brown, a new prebendary was appointed in the person of the Reverend Frederick George Bennett, D.C.L. The following year Bishop Durnford, with the assent of the Dean and Chapter and the Prebendary, made fresh statutes, which, as they did not prove entirely satisfactory, were modified in 1887. As a result of these measures all scholars were in future to pay fees, which were not, however, to exceed £15 a year; boys joining the school had to be over eight years old and were required to pass an entrance examination; and the Dean and Chapter were entitled to nominate cathedral scholars at reduced fees provided that their number did not constitute more than one eighth of the whole school. These were additional to the choristers, whose fees the Dean and Chapter undertook to pay.

Instruction was to be given in Latin, Greek, French, Mathematics and the English subjects, but German, Science, Music and Drawing were to be treated as extras. The fact that the Dean and Chapter were empowered to license boarding houses suggests that boarding on the premises was at this stage temporarily discontinued.

Among the thirty-nine children in attendance at this time was H. W. Chase, who was a pupil here from 1884 to 1890 and has left some lively reminiscences of his years at the Prebendal School.

'With what fear and trepidation', he writes, 'I made my first entry into the old school. It was a fine May morning, though still somewhat cold, and luckily for me a Saint's day—St Philip and St James—and consequently a half-holiday. My brother, an older and much stronger boy, had preceded me by a few days as I had unfortunately been unwell. I was neither choir boy nor boarder, but just an ordinary day boy.

'The lesson, which, of course, I had not prepared, was in divinity, and I took my allotted place at the bottom of a class of about a dozen or more small boys under the third master, Mr. C. Pierpont Edwards. I should have said that on arrival I was cheered at being hailed by at least one boy whom I knew as a pupil at an earlier school.

'I remember being sufficiently awed by the prefects, who, distinguished by wearing "mortar-boards", kept order until the arrival of the masters. My awe was deepened by the entry of the preceptors, who were in the full glory of 'varsity gowns and of course wearing or carrying their "mortar-boards". The headmaster was the Rev. Prebendary F. G. Bennett, B.C.L., a former assistant master at Hurstpierpoint College, whose kindness and sympathy I soon learned to appreciate. The second master was Mr. W. H. Woodward, whose after career I have never been able to learn. He was somewhat reserved and was rather feared than liked. The third, Mr. Edwards, I have already mentioned. He afterwards took holy orders and was sometimes known in the press as the "fighting parson", though he was probably not the only priest to whom the epithet has been applied.

'To go back to the lesson, I well remember that it was from the gospel story of the prodigal son and I made my first step upward by answering the question: "Who told him?" (i.e. the father) by giving the correct answer, which the boy standing above me in the class had failed to do. But I am forgetting to say that the first business was the calling of the roll by one of the prefects, followed by a reading from the Bible, a psalm or psalms and prayers. The prayers were, of course, conducted by the head, whose devout care in doing so was noticeable. How I used to enjoy his reading of the 68th Psalm and I never hear it today without a thought of him and, curiously enough, of Cromwell at Dunbar. Then being a Saint's Day and the lesson over, we all went to the cathedral for morning prayer. Then back to school for a short time and the rest of the day was ours. I think the afternoon was spent in practising cricket in Priory Park, our cricketing materials being stored in the old priory. I little realised then that this fine building was but a fragment—the choir (chancel)—of a much larger monastery church. The building after the dissolution had served various purposes—a Guildhall, Town Hall and later a court of justice. The high seats for the judges were still in existence when I first remember the place—pretentious thrones of poor quality, covered with some sort of red cloth, with desks etc. to match. The rifle volunteers in their grey uniform and armed with the Snider rifle also used the building.

'The curriculum at the school comprised divinity, grammar, arithmetic, geometry, algebra, history, poetry, Latin, French, geography and physical geography. A very few scholars also took Greek. No drawing was taught save as an extra and I remember only one instance of this. There was a certain amount of drill taught by a sergeant from the barracks, but it was dropped soon after I came on the scene and for some reason I was never taught any. Possibly it was for boarders only.

'Examinations were held from time to time—I forget their frequency—and all was done in writing save the declamation exam. In the latter case, we were called in turn—as a class—from an adjoining room in the headmaster's house and had to stand upon a small platform at the headmaster's desk. A cue was then given us by the headmaster from the lower end of the room and we were expected immediately to proceed and repeat from whatever poem or play we had been taught during the preceding session. One remembers the short miscellany of the lower class, Scott's *Lady of the Lake* or *Lay of the Last Minstrel*, perhaps in the second form, and Shakespeare's plays in the first or upper form. Boys were much more nervous then and I well remember one lad (not myself) who always ended in a flood of tears, though he was said to be a capital horseman and took part in horse jumping exhibitions. As a dayboy, I had not the run of the place and had only access to the entrance passage, then partly cobbled with seashore boulders and having, I think, stone slabs in the middle, the lobby where we stowed our caps etc., the actual schoolroom, and, for sanitary purposes only, the garden. There an antiquated row of privies, whose wooden partitions were adorned with hundreds of carved names or initials, would have given rise to astonishment to any modern sanitary inspector. On the way thither we passed through an outhouse wherein stood a curious old pump. I do not remember that any provision was there made for ablutions, but doubtless the boarders were better provided.

'The schoolroom, well lighted at one end (the south), was somewhat dark in the middle and improved again in this respect at the north end. There was but one blackboard and that was fixed to the wall. I remember no maps or other pictures as having been hanging on the walls, but the headmaster's throne, still, I believe, in existence, was a fine old carved chair which Mr. Bennett once told me he thought to be Jacobean. There were about ten monitors' or upper pupils' desks, probably of oak or mahogany, two of which were near the head's desk. All were adorned with innumerable carved initials or names of scholars—so much so that writing on them was a matter of some difficulty.

'We wore pillbox peakless caps of dark material with the badge of the arms of the see of Chichester on them (not the badge at pesent worn by the boys) varied by straw "boaters" with a scarlet (or red), black and white silk band. The prefects' "mortar-boards" were discontinued soon after my arrival upon the the ground of expense. For cricket we mostly had our "whites", but a few were possessors of a peaked cricket cap of red (or scarlet) and black in stripes and possibly a "blazer" to match.

'I am hazy about the football colours as I only played once or twice—in my ordinary clothes—and was excused from further participation on the grounds of delicate health. This game was played on a field, now built upon, which was entered from what is now called Market Avenue, then Market Road. The trees were planted at a later time. The same field was used for our annual school sports and was provided with a poor windowless shed or storehouse. As the field abutted on an allotment field at one end and had also a pond on one side of it, which often received the ball, and the goals being merely uprights of wood with white tape stretched across the tops, it can be seen that, in the total absence of goal nets, the conditions were far from ideal.

'A Monsieur A. Buquet came into the school about once a week to take an upper French class. He was dapper and most amiable, a fact of which I fear advantage was taken to the detriment of our progress.'

Writing elsewhere of Prebendary Bennett, for whom he had a healthy respect and affection, Mr. Chase recalls that:

'He had a great interest—not to say love—of boys and of him no boy ever spoke ill. Majestic in appearance, with "muttonchop" side whiskers and a twinkling eye, wearing a monocle and a 'varsity gown over black clothes, he is still my ideal of what a schoolmaster ought to be. He was a married man, with one little girl, whom I remember to have seen watching with him the boys crowding into the then cobbled passage leading from West Street into the school. "Aren't they funny beasts!" he would say with a smile to the child.

'Always maintaining discipline, he enlivened our lessons with a good many jokes and gave boys nicknames like "Petropoloski", but from him there could be no offence. Like Dr. Johnson, he professed to prefer southerners to those from north of the Tweed, saying jokingly that Scotland was a place were on Sundays "they pulled down the blinds and drank whisky inside!" This, like Johnson's view, was evidently not to be taken seriously.

'After a short time, I had overcome my fear of merciless whippings and, as a matter of fact, I never experienced a thrashing. One fine day Mr. Bennett pulled his desk drawer open before me, saying, "You see what is in there, don't you?" "Yes, sir", I replied. "Then you must work", he said. The warning was enough, my lessons were learned and I began to enjoy history, divinity, and poetry, though shewing very poor progress in Mathematics.'

In fact, Chase went on to win a succession of prizes for history, divinity and declamation. In a revealing reference to the composition of the school, he recollects that there were in his time about thirty boys, of whom a dozen or so were boarders. This suggests that the numbers were already declining again by 1890. By the time that Prebendary Bennett's thirty-three-year-long reign came to an end in 1912 the school is alleged to have been catering virtually for the choristers only. Five years earlier the *Victoria County History* had ruefully concluded its article on the Prebendal School with the observation that 'for all practical purposes Chichester contains no public secondary school of a high grade'.

Chapter Five

DISPERSAL AND REUNIFICATION: 1914–31

IT IS DIFFICULT, even at a mere seventy years remove, to arrive at a satisfactory explanation why, when the school was at such a low ebb, it was considered necessary to split it down the middle, but the fact remains that, soon after the outbreak of the first World War, the choristers were transferred to a separate building in another part of the city. Even so the numbers who continued to be educated under the old roof were up to forty in September 1915 and under Prebendary William Pearce, M.A., who had succeeded Bennet on the latter's retirement, they rose to sixty-two in January 1917. This was partly due to the return of a Mr. Moore, who had previously taught eighteen years at the Prebendal School in Bennett's time, and who now brought eleven of his own pupils with him.

Though, paper being in short supply, the *Prebendalian* was a slender and infrequent publication, its pages reflect the conflict raging across the Channel. There are lists of Old Boys serving in the armed forces, letters from the front line and, all too predictably, announcements of casualties. The Reverend C. Pierpont Edwards, whom Mr. Chase remembered as third master in 1884, was commended for going on with a funeral service in Gallipoli while shrapnel burst over the mourners. 'After quietly pronouncing the Benediction he proceeded to bandage a wounded man who had fallen at the graveside.'

An important feature of the school at this time was its Scout troop, which was given regular instruction in ambulance work by Mr. Cole, himself an Old Prebendalian, and undertook spells of duty at Graylingwell Military

Hospital, for which many of the boys received war service badges.

Understandably, sporting fixtures with other schools were difficult to arrange. Too often it was a case of the boarders challenging the dayboys, but the magazine records occasional matches against the Lancastrians and Colebrook, Bognor, and more regular encounters with the Bluecoats and the Choir School. In the autumn of 1915 the Prebendal boys won their football match against the choristers by 10 goals to nil and in the following summer they were equally successful in beating the choir boys at cricket, when stumps were drawn with six wickets to spare, but these results are scarcely surprising when one remembers that the Prebendal had twice as many boys from whom to select their players.

The choristers were now based on a building in Northgate which had formerly been a dame school. It had long rows of wooden steps on which the infants had once sat, and the boys occupied large oak desks, much carved with initials. Outside there was a playground, which adjoined St Paul's churchyard.

The headmaster of the choir school was Mr. H. E. Ball (R.N. retired), who held this position from the school's opening until his retirement in 1929, and was assisted from 1926 onwards by Mr. (later the Rev.) Malcolm Methuen Clarke. The latter had been a Chichester chorister from 1918 until 1924 and was to teach, both at Northgate and subsequently in West Street, for seven years before going up to King's College, Cambridge. He was later to become an honorary canon of Peterborough.

The timetable at the choir school had inevitably to be geared on every day except Thursday, which was known as 'dumb day', to Mattins at 10.00 a.m. and Evensong at 4.15 p.m. Taking account of the need for daily practices, which probably took place between 9.00 and 10.00 a.m., the time left for lessons was lamentably short, as all had to be squeezed into the latter half of the morning and the early part of the afternoon. In effect school hours were from 11.00 a.m. to 1.00 p.m. and from 2.00 p.m. to 3.45 p.m., so in the winter months there can have been no daylight hours left for games.

Under these arrangements much time must have been wasted by the choristers having to walk the length of North Street four times a day, which they did in crocodile and wearing Eton suits and black 'mortar-boards' with red tassels.

When in 1929 Mr. Ball retired, the new Dean, the Very Reverend Arthur Stuart Duncan-Jones, became titular Head, but left the organisation and day-to-day supervision of the school to Mr. Methuen Clarke, who remained as the Housemaster in charge.

Meanwhile, because numbers had fallen sharply, the Prebendal School had been forced to close its doors and the premises on West Street were standing empty. One of those who was still in attendance when this happened was Mr. Dorian Prince, who, after qualifying as an architect and serving in the Royal Engineers during the second World War, emigrated to New Zealand. He recollects that in 1924 there were sixty-nine boys and three masters—Prebendary Pearce, Mr. Moore (known as 'Grasshopper') and Mr. Tolman—yet by 1928 the numbers had dropped to 33, with but the first two masters in charge.

'The old buildings', he writes, 'were frightfully decrepit, the toilets unmentionable and sport a farce. We played cricket in a meadow near where St Margaret's Hospital now stands [the writer, looking back over a period of fifty years, may well be confused over names and locations], and before each game we had to shovel up the cowpats and cut the pitch with a hand mower from grass and buttercups about twelve inches high. Hardly conducive to high scores, but of great assistance to the bowlers! Other memories are of cold hours spent in the cathedral on Saints' Days, compensated by a half-day holiday, and the Empire Day parades in Priory Park.'

Now the conjunction of three elements—a choir school that lacked a convenient base, vacant buildings hard by the cathedral, and the appointment in 1929 of a Dean with a keen interest in education—were to lead to a realistic appraisal of the available options and a scheme that would both cater for the schooling of the choristers and preserve those links with the past that were inherent in the title—Prebendal School.

The upshot was that the buildings on West Street were extensively restored, No. 53 being assigned as living accommodation for the teaching, catering and domestic staff, and in 1931 the school formally re-opened with Dean Duncan-Jones, now Prebendary of Highleigh, as its headmaster in fact as well as in name. Thus the Prebendal School and the Choir School were once more united under one roof.

At the outset only four boys were living in, but gradually the old system of farming out was abandoned and the number of boarders rose to twenty, all choristers or probationers. In addition there were a few dayboys from the city and district. The staff consisted of the headmaster and three others—the Rev. Donald Manners, a former chorister who became chaplain, Mr. H. E. Ball, and Mr. Methuen Clarke. Mr. Clarke's parents moved into No. 53 West Street with him, as did his sister, Irene (later Mrs. Russell Purchase), and they were granted various concessions in terms of board and lodging, as Mr. Methuen Clarke's mother acted as unpaid matron, cook and caterer.

Since the income from the school's endowment was at this time little more than £130 per annum, and the cost of renovating and refurnishing the buildings amounted to more than £1,400, the Dean arranged for a substantial loan from the Ecclesiastical Commissioners and at the same time launched an appeal which was directed to Old Prebendalians and ex-choristers, but also resulted in a generous gift from the widow of Frederick John Read (Cathedral Organist from 1921 to 1925) for the provision of a playing field. This was situated on land bought from the Church Commissioners in Westgate Fields and was augmented by the erection of a cricket pavilion, for which Methuen Clarke had raised the necessary £600 in a separate appeal.

The first prospectus, issued in 1931, was a single-leaf folder and in its economically worded description of the establishment defines it as a preparatory boarding school for boys aged eight to fifteen. The boarding fees were £75 per annum, with special rates for sons of clergy; for probationers these were reduced to £45 per annum, and for choristers to £35 per annum; while dayboys were admitted for five guineas per term. At that time dayboys were eligible to be choristers and, in the event of their being taken into the choir, they received their education free of charge.

Though it was not until 1935 that the Statutes were revised, a new course had been charted and, thanks to the vision and faith of Dean Duncan-Jones, the Prebendal School was reborn.

Chapter Six

THE PREPARATORY SCHOOL: 1931–51

AT CHRISTMAS 1931 Mr. Ball, having seen the new school safely launched, resumed his interrupted retirement and was replaced by Mr. P. C. Manwaring, who had but recently left Ardingly, where he was Head of School. In addition to teaching English and History he coached games and soon came to be known affectionately as Sam.

It was in this same year that Dr. Harvey Grace became the cathedral organist and choir master and that the Dean and he decided to replace the choristers' red cassocks by grey cassocks with wide puritan collars. The red had been worn since the year 1902 or thereabouts, having been introduced by an earlier organist, F. J. W. Crowe, who always insisted that the cathedral was a royal foundation.

Dr. Grace took his place on the House Committee which at this time regulated the affairs of the school and he was instrumental in rearranging the times of morning lessons, which were now to run from nine o'clock to noon. It was also at this juncture that the choristers' Eton suits and 'mortar-boards' were abandoned in favour of coats and shorts in grey tweed, which were worn with matching grey shirts, stockings and pullovers by all Prebendalians. The new suits were offset by a scarlet cap with a badge based on the arms of Bishop Story.

The Minutes of the House Committee in these early years show all too clearly that the school was operating on a shoe-string. When the matron requested a new brush and shovel for the fireplace, one was granted, but not the other; the cricket pitch was rolled by the boys with a roller borrowed from the Bishop; and consideration was given to the

27

possibility of mowing the field 'with the help of a small car attached to the existing mower'. The installation of a telephone had to wait for some years and the total amount that could be allocated to fire precautions was limited to £20.

In 1933 Mr. Methuen Clarke went up to Cambridge and was replaced by Mr. David Duncan-Jones. At the same time his parents and sister moved to a house of their own, necessitating the appointment of a new matron in the person of Mrs. Helen Garrett. Further changes ensued in 1935 following the alterations of the Statutes, for at this stage the Dean took the title of Warden and appointed the young Mr. Manwaring to the headmastership with a Mr. Byard as assistant master. There were now thirty-nine boys in the school—about the average for preparatory schools between the wars—so good housekeeping and careful husbandry were clearly reaping their reward.

According to R. B. Elliott, who was admitted as a chorister at Michaelmas 1933, there were some ten or a dozen boys sleeping in the main dormitory (i.e., Long Dormitory) and about four older boys in the annexe (now known as Tarring Dormitory).

'Beneath the dormitory', he recalls, 'was the library and music room. The walls were all books and the floor was almost covered by a very long table, but there was sufficient room for a black upright piano at the north end. Also at that end was a door to the landing. The "Remove" was just across the landing, which would mean it was under the annexe. Both the library and the "Remove" were used as classrooms. A window in the west wall, but at the north end of the library [i.e., in what is now St Richard's Dormitory] overlooked a small garden in which there were a few ancient fruit trees. The wall on the west side of the garden separated us from a garage. I vaguely remember the hand-operated petrol pump and its gantry which was pulled out to bridge the pavement and fed fuel at 1s. 3d. per gallon to the likes of the H.M., who had a scarlet and cream sports car, or Canon Russell's big black saloon. [Canon Russell taught divinity at the school.]

'The room beneath the library has not changed much, except that its two classroom areas were only separated by a hinged screen about six feet or so in height. The north end was always used for Art, which meant pencil copying of black and white printed pictures of farmyard and other rural scenes. Under this classroom was the basement. This was the place where we boarders played about when the weather was inclement, during weekends or in the evenings. It had an earth floor. During my time we acquired a set of parallel bars, a high bar and a couple of suspended ropes for climbing. I don't recall any serious accidents in spite of the hair-raising stunts that were attempted without any adult supervision.

'The kitchen was then where it is now and the two dining-rooms, one for boarders and the other for day-boys' lunch, lay between the boys' school entrance passage and the front door to the private side [now sealed and incorporated within the domestic staff dining-room].

'Immediately to the south of the school building was a cinder yard, used as a playground, but now covered by recent extensions.

'I recall the installation of an emergency fire escape unit in the south window of the main dormitory. This comprised an adjustable belt attached to a friction drum. We boys made great fun of initial tests, disappearing over the window ledge showing an unbalanced mixture of exhilaration and stupefied paralysis. On one such occasion one of our number was left suspended somewhere below the library window for a while because of a temporary hitch with the cord on the drum.'

The organist in Ralph Elliott's time was, of course, Dr. Harvey Grace. The choristers do not appear to have seen much of him, but Ralph Elliott vaguely recollects him as 'a pleasant though firm, grey-haired old gentleman of rather rotund proportions'. In those days it was Mr. O'Connor

(known to the boys as Paddy) who was always in charge of
the choir. 'He was a fiery fellow', writes Ralph Elliott, 'not
bad natured, but very quick-tempered and not averse to
using his baton as an immediate remedy for a wrong note or
some other indiscretion'.

Although the outbreak of the second World War in 1939
occasioned inevitable problems of staffing and the sort of
hardships associated with wartime, the school continued to
function without interruption. Mr. Manwaring, being of an age
at which he was liable for military service, was duly called up,
but the Dean requested deferment, which was granted. When at
length it became necessary for him to enlist, he was allowed
frequent weekend leave in order to keep an eye on the school,
but in his absence it was Dean Duncan-Jones who held the reins
as acting headmaster. This was not a role for which temperament or his training had prepared him, so in practice most of
the day-to-day administration, at least from 1944 onwards,
was shared between Mrs. Eve Salwey (the late Mrs. Eve
Powell) and, until he, too, was called up, Mr. Peter Head.

Chichester, by virtue of its geographical position—close
to R.A.F. Tangmere and the Naval Dockyard at Portsmouth—
was often overflown by German bombers and suffered
damage when bombs were offloaded over the city. Mrs.
Powell, who at Mr. Manwaring's request lived in for a term,
recalls how, as soon as the air-raid sirens sounded, staff and
pupils all trooped down to the cellar. When this happened
at night, they spent quite long periods below ground,
wrapped in blankets and drinking tea, while the adults did
their best to keep the children happy.

Rations at this stage were adequate, but there were few
luxuries. 'During my term of living in', writes Mrs. Powell,
'we had no cook, so I had to feed boys and staff. I would rise
early, cook breakfast, then take my first teaching period
before rushing into the kitchen to prepare lunch. After
eleven o'clock I had time to set work for my boys, but not
to stay with them, because I then had to cook a main dish
and a pudding for everyone. The evening meal was basic—
piles of bread and butter, not much of the latter, and jam if
the ration held out'.

When hostilities ceased, there was one term during which the school was run by Mr. P. E. Ellard-Handley, but thereafter from 1945 to 1951 the headmaster was the Dean's son, the Rev. A. R. Duncan-Jones, who had previously taught at the school in the autumn of 1932.

The staff at this juncture consisted of the headmaster himself, Mrs. Salwey and the two Priest Vicars, one of whom, the Rev. A. E. Fost, taught French. Though she had no professional qualifications at all, Mrs. Salwey was a very successful teacher of English. 'In particular', Mr. Duncan-Jones recollects, 'she aroused in the upper forms a remarkable enthusiasm for Shakespeare—and the tragedies at that. I remember robustly defending her against narrow-minded inspectors or "educationalists" who protested that it wasn't suitable pabulum for young boys. But then I would: for it was my own practice then and to the end of my teaching days to make my twelve-year-olds learn large chunks of Virgil by heart!'

When Mr. Duncan-Jones arrived, there were about thirty-six boys in the school. 'The governing body had just with some trepidation raised the fees by £5 to £85 a year. Half way through my first year I put it to them that the fees must go up to £120. Consternation! I recall Canon Crosse, Prebendary of Highleigh and Headmaster of Ardingly, saying, "You are proposing an increase of 40 per cent. Have you a waiting list?" To which I replied, "No, and I never shall have until I charge a reasonable fee." They agreed. And in the same term (September 1946) that the fee went up by 40 per cent the numbers went up by 50 per cent. Of course it was a moment when anyone who was not actually blind, halt or withered could fill a prep. school. By the time I left I think the numbers were between 60 and 70.'

The increase in the number of boys necessitated some expansion in the accommodation available and the need was met in 1947 by the acquisition of No. 54 West Street, which had historically been occupied by the Sub-Dean and had latterly served as St Peter's vicarage. In the autumn of 1946, when the building was standing empty and before the work of converting it had begun, fire broke out on the first floor.

The gardener had put a large log to burn on one of the grates, with the purpose of drying the house, and it fell out and set fire to the floor. Happily, however, the new building was ready for occupation by the September term and made a great difference in the way of providing staff accommodation, dormitories and bathrooms.

At the same time, through the good offices of Canon Lowther Clarke, the proprietors of Hymns Ancient and Modern, of whom he was one, purchased for the school the strip of garden that faces the west door of the cathedral and is now known as the Memorial Garden. A stone commemorates old pupils who gave their lives in the two world wars and there is a handsome wrought-iron gate in the archway.

These extensions were formally opened by H.R.H. The Duchess of Kent when she came to the special service held in the cathedral to celebrate the 450th anniversary of the school's refoundation. Princess Marina planted a willow tree against the southern boundary wall (it unfortunately died of willow disease in about 1971), and, as Mr. Duncan-Jones recalls, the preacher on this occasion was Canon Spencer Leeson, formerly Headmaster of Winchester College and then Vicar of St Mary's, Southampton, 'who, with his customary gift for hyperbole, declared in his sermon that the Prebendal School "took rank among the greatest and noblest in the land".'

It was also in Mr. Duncan-Jones's time that the school acquired the main garden connecting the west end of the Memorial Garden with the city wall where it now abuts upon the Avenue de Chartres. This was originally part of the Bishop's garden and, as such, belonged to the Church Commissioners. Not long afterwards an unsatisfactory and antiquated outside lavatory was replaced by a new changing-room block projecting southwards from the school kitchen. At its southern end it is overhung by a weeping lime (or tree of heaven) planted by Mr. Duncan-Jones with the particular intention of obscuring the view of the red brick factory building in West Street for anyone coming through the wrought-iron gate from the Cathedral. (The building in question has since been demolished.)

'It may be interesting', writes Mr. Duncan-Jones, 'to recall what short holidays the choristers had in those days. At Christmas they stayed until Epiphany or the Sunday after, for they always took part in the great Epiphany Procession, when hundreds of schoolchildren, four or six deep, carried candles round the cathedral to the [recorder] accompaniment of the Dolmetsches. After that the choristers had one Sunday off, i.e., the inside of a fortnight. They had the same after Easter or Low Sunday; and four Sundays off in the summer—when choirs from around the diocese commonly came and sang. This regimen, so monstrous to modern ears, was of course not felt as any hardship by the boys, as anyone familiar with choristers will know. It *could* be described as a hardship to the Headmaster and matron-housekeeper, both of whom have much to do between one term and the next, but I don't think we repined. There was much enthusiasm'.

It was in 1947 or 1948 that the school enlisted the services of George Fuller, a retired cricket pro living in Chichester, to come and coach the boys. He was, as Mr. Duncan-Jones describes him, 'a wonderful personality. Everybody hung on his words as he reminisced about such legendary figures as Hobbs and Compton. He came three or four afternoons a week and insisted that not only the 1st XI but every boy should pass through his hands at least once a week. As a result our cricket was, for a small school, very good'. In this connection it is worthy of note that throughout his six years at the school it was the Headmaster himself who acted as groundsman, taking considerable pride in the quality of the games field.

The staff had earlier been augmented by the appointment as an assistant of Mr. C. E. Fance, a London primary school head teacher who had just retired and whom Mr. Duncan-Jones remembers as 'a jolly, hearty, spherical little man and in an old-fashioned way an immensely thorough teacher of all basic subjects at primary level'. His wife combined the jobs of matron and housekeeper, but soon found that the work was too much for her to undertake single-handed, so a series of assistant matrons was engaged. One of those who was appointed to this post was Miss Jean Mackenzie, who was married to Mr. Duncan-Jones in 1951 and took over the jobs of matron and housekeeper, for Mr. Fance suffered a stroke and he and his wife had to give up working. The Fances had enjoyed the use of the big room overlooking the garden as their sitting-room and this now became the Headmaster's study, which it remained until the summer of 1982. 'Its only drawback', Mr. Duncan-Jones recollects, 'was that the room underneath was used for music and, since it housed the Hurdis organ, was known as the Hurdis Room. The little rooms beyond were also music practice rooms, so that my daytime thoughts were not entirely undisturbed. Indeed I recall that in my last term, when I was engaged to be married, the favourite piece of one of our young organists was Mendelssohn's "Wedding March", and he was always playing this on the Hurdis organ—sublimely unconscious of its aptness.'

Mr. Duncan-Jones had originally been appointed at the suggestion of the Precentor, Canon Browne-Wilkinson, for a period of 'two years or so', to set the school on its feet after the war, but in the event he had been in office for six years when in 1951 he and Mrs. Duncan-Jones took ship for Bombay, where he was to become Chaplain of St Thomas's Cathedral and of All Saints' Church. His place as headmaster was for two years filled by the Rev. Charles H. Sinclair, M.A.

It was in Mr. Sinclair's time that the school received its first full inspection by H.M.I., and it was he who introduced Rugby Football as a Lent Term activity. Although the first team that the school fielded in 1952 was patently lacking in experience, it must have made up for this in resolution and vitality to have won its first match (against Westbourne House) by 11-0—a *tour de force* that does not appear to have been repeated. Boxing matches against Oakwood had been on the school calendar for some years, but 1952 was equally memorable on this front for being the first year in which the Prebendal School won. Perhaps this was the result of the introduction of boxing colours and a special tie, which were first awarded to Simon Stoodley and Nigel Purchase for their performance in the ring on this occasion.

In 1952 the *Prebendalian* records that 'as in previous years, the Choir took part in the British Legion's Festival of Remembrance at the Albert Hall', and in the following summer it tells how the Cathedral and Diocese celebrated the seventh centenary of the death of St Richard of Chichester. 'Four of our boys', runs the article, 'took part in "The Acts of St Richard", a pageant performed on four days in the forecourt of the Bishop's Palace. We were all present at the High Mass in the Cathedral on June 13th, when the Archbishop of Canterbury was the celebrant; and the choristers were invited to the Civic Luncheon, at which His Grace was entertained, and sang the grace before the meal'.

In the autumn of that year Mr. Guy F. Hepburn, M.A., succeeded Mr. Sinclair as Headmaster. There were then 72 boys in the school, of whom 50 were boarding. Numbers therefore had doubled in a period of eight years.

Chapter Seven

DEVELOPMENTS: 1953-69

IN RECENT YEARS it has not, for a variety of possible reasons, been so easy to find good choristers as was once the case. For all the liberality of deans and chapters in financing choral scholarships that are index-linked, inflation must be held largely to blame, but in the spring of 1954 prices and likewise school fees were still relatively stable and no fewer than twenty-five candidates presented themselves at the Voice Trials.

That year Bishop Bell was granted the Freedom of the City and the Very Reverend A. S. Duncan-Jones celebrated his Silver Jubilee as Dean, the choristers singing at both the banquets that were held in their honour. Sadly, however, the Dean was not to enjoy any further anniversaries, for he died in office on 19 January 1955.

Mr. Hepburn, looking back on their brief association, summons up a picture of a dignitary who belonged in character to an earlier century; he recalls a man who was at once kind and forceful and one for whom there was great respect. It is not perhaps too fanciful to attribute the survival of the school to him and there can be no doubt that it benefited in untold ways from his unflagging care and concern for its welfare.

Following the death of Dean Duncan-Jones the most significant event of the year 1955 took place in November when a team of H.M.I., led by Mr. Frank Birks, paid the school a second visit and were sufficiently impressed to recommend that it should receive official recognition from the Ministry of Education. This was accorded early in the following year, and it is worthy of note that, when Mr. Birks subsequently

36

retired from Her Majesty's Inspectorate, he accepted an invitation from the new Dean (The Very Rev. J. Walter A. Hussey) to become a governor of the school (technically a lay adviser to the governors). From 1967 to 1977, when illness compelled him to resign his place on the board, his wisdom and experience in the field of education were to prove invaluable in promoting sound academic standards and in helping to build a reputation for the place.

At the end of the Christmas Term in 1955 Mrs. Salwey left after eleven years' service to the school, and a year later the Rev. A. E. Fost, who had given thirteen years to the Cathedral and school, retired to become Vicar of Burpham.

It was a time when, as the inspectors' report testified, the school was doing well scholastically and was also pre-eminent in sport.

'We were unbeaten', Mr. Hepburn records, 'in four rugger matches and won six out of eight at cricket, our captain, John Horton, being presented with a new ball by the London *Evening Star* for scoring 50 and taking six wickets in one match.' The Prebendal School also succeeded in winning the first two of a series of Triangular Athletics events which had been instituted with Westbourne House and Avisford the previous year. (They became Quadrangular events when Great Ballard joined in 1964.) Since the school did not then have a swimming pool among its facilities, there were occasional excursions to West Wittering, where the headmaster bought a hut on the beach. This was to prove particularly useful during choir holidays.

It was choir holiday time when on 30 July 1956 Her Majesty the Queen and H.R.H. the Duke of Edinburgh visited the city. The choristers sang at the service in the Cathedral and were well placed afterwards to give the royal visitors a good send-off. They received a letter from the Mayor and Corporation congratulating them on their singing and their conduct, and this was framed and hung in the school dining-hall. Recalling the occasion, Mr. Hepburn says: 'There had been a violent storm the night before and Priory Park, where events were to begin, was—to put it mildly —in a mess. The Mayor, Mr. Leslie Evershed-Martin, put out an appeal on the national radio in the early morning, asking any citizen who could manage to do so to turn up at the Park to help clear up. The Headmaster of the High School, Mr. Anderson, and I, duly turned up, but, if anyone else did, we failed to observe them!'

In 1957 the school took over No. 1 St Richard's Walk, which provided two good classrooms and some quite extensive accommodation for staff, enabling various rooms in the main block to be put to other purposes, including an Art Room overlooking West Street.

At this juncture the school numbered ninety-six boys (75 boarders and 21 dayboys), which represented an increase of 26 pupils over a period of four years.

At Christmas (1957) Mr. Hepburn left to become Headmaster of Eastbourne College Preparatory School and was succeeded in January 1958 by the Reverend Bernard P. Bate, who was previously Precentor of Norwich and as such had been attached to the staff of King Edward VI School (now Norwich School).

Mr. Bate was to be Headmaster for the next eleven years and during this time he was responsible for a number of innovations. Soon after his arrival in Chichester the small dormitory at the top of No. 53 West Street and adjoining the dormitory called Tarring was converted into two rooms for the matrons, and a television set was acquired for the Selden Room, which also served as the school library and boarders' common room, but much more significant changes were in the offing.

In 1961 the installation of an electric kiln in the kitchen of No. 1 St Richard's Walk enabled pottery to be introduced to the curriculum, and in 1966 carpentry classes were started beneath the headmaster's house in one of the cellars, which was converted into a workshop. In the following year, as Mr. Bate had abolished boxing as a school activity, the old boxing cellar below the thirteenth-century schoolhouse was turned into a recreation room, where the boarders could amuse themselves with games of table tennis, billiards, monopoly, or chess. With a touch of irony, in view of the way in which boys tend to handle equipment, it came to be known as the rec. (pronounced 'wreck') room.

In 1967 a Science Laboratory was opened in the east wing of the Bishop's Palace, which the school had begun to lease from the Church Commissioners two years earlier, when the Theological College, having erected a new building on its Westgate site, no longer required the premises. This step reflected the growing importance of Science in the Common Entrance Examination, where it was shortly to oust Latin as a compulsory subject. Though the available equipment was somewhat basic, it enabled boys to embark on the Nuffield Science course with Mr. Bate, who taught the subject himself.

With the acquisition of this new teaching and residential accommodation, the school no longer had need of No. 1 St Richard's Walk, which reverted to private occupation, but the room on the ground floor (now part of the Bishop Bell Rooms) was retained as an Art Room.

The Old Kitchen of the Bishop's Palace was not included in the terms of the lease since it was used from time to time by clergy and visiting choirs, and occasionally housed exhibitions of one kind of another, but in practice the school was more often than not permitted by the Bishop to make use of the room for morning assemblies, music lessons, concerts and plays. The latter, which had usually been presented in the extremely confined area of the school room on West Street, now gained considerably in scope and range. In fact the annual school play, ably produced and skilfully costumed by Mrs. Diana Bate, rapidly became one of the highlights of the year and attained a remarkably high standard for preparatory school productions.

Meanwhile there had been equally striking developments in the sporting facilities available to the school. First and foremost was the erection in 1961 of a freestanding Purley swimming pool of timber and plastic at the western extremity of the school garden, where it was sheltered on three sides by ancient flint walls and on the fourth by a beech hedge.

'Not long after the original swimming pool was completed', Mr. Bate remembers, 'I answered the telephone and the voice at the other end said, "This is the editor of the *Times* newspaper speaking. I have got on my desk a photograph of the west end of Chichester Cathedral taken with your swimming pool in the foreground. It is such a lovely picture that I am ringing you to ask if I might send our official photographer to take a picture for publication". Of course I said "Yes!" and soon after this a huge picture appeared on the back page of the *Times.*'

What the school signally lacked, as it still does, was a gymnasium. It was therefore most unfortunate that, when the Oliver Whitby School was closed down and its relatively modern gymnasium block was offered to the Prebendal, the governors felt unable to seize the opportunity, and the building subsequently became a G.P.O. sorting office.

The absence of such indoor facilities was keenly felt during the long, hard winter of 1962–63. According to Mr. Keith Ross (now Senior Master at the Pilgrims' School, Winchester), who had just joined the staff, 'it started to snow on either Christmas night or Boxing Day night and once a decent covering of snow had established itself, the weather grew colder and colder, so cold in fact that, on returning to our quarters at No. 1 St Richard's Walk after the holidays, Noel Osborne and I found the bath, which had somehow filled itself half full of water, had frozen solid. The playing fields were very soon out of action, as we quickly tired of throwing snow (or ice) at each other, and it was then that the Archdeacon, the Ven. Lancelot Mason (I think) came up with the idea of our using the Cloisters as an exercise area'. With the Dean's consent the suggestion was adopted—'the only time', says Mr. Bate, 'that the Cloisters had been used for the purpose in 600 years!' Bishop Richard Praty in his visitation of 1441 had peremptorily forbidden games of ball and other sports carried on by children in the cloisters and graveyard.

The 1963 issue of the *Prebendalian* reports that the games 'provided ample opportunity for improvisation. Rules were invented or abandoned according to temperament or temperature. Basketball (no basket), Netball (no net) and Rugby (no ball) were among the most popular, though one school of thought preferred relay-races. Injuries were only minor, and relatively few excursions were made into Paradise, and these only to collect stray tennis balls, while windows cracked and timbers shivered'.

'It must', says Mr. Ross, 'have been the Clerk of Works who commented afterwards that the glass in the windows of the cloisters had survived two World Wars, not to mention the worst excesses of Cromwell's days, but that no power on earth could protect it from Prebendalians.' In fact, Mr. Bate is confident that in all those hair-raising weeks only one small, clear pane of glass was broken.

When work began in 1964 on the creation of a new inner ring road—the present Avenue de Chartres—across Westgate Fields, the school had to vacate its normal playing field, being offered instead the use of the Orchard Street ground. It was not until 1966 that the school was able to claim possession of its new field, which was the land between the new road and the Lavant course, and it was two years later that the new prefabricated cricket pavilion was put up in the corner formed by the bend in the stream.

In the interlude, as a result of the fund-raising efforts of parents, staff and pupils, two grass tennis courts had been laid in the Deanery paddock, to which the school had access for games. At Speech Day that year (1966) the Dean, whose garden overlooked the courts, offered to sell the following year, at a reduced price, used Prebendal tennis balls.

This was a period of great development in the musical activities of both Cathedral and school. Following the retirement in 1958 of Mr. Horace A. Hawkins ('Hawkie' to the boys), who had been Organist for twenty years, Mr. John Birch was appointed from All Saints', Margaret Street, to be Organist and Master of the Choristers, and he was joined in July 1961 by Mr. Richard Seal (Organist and Master of the Choristers at Salisbury Cathedral since 1968), who became Assistant Organist and Director of Music at the Prebendal School.

In 1960 the Southern Cathedrals Festival (Winchester, Salisbury and Chichester) was revived, the first cathedral to host the event being Winchester. As was the case before the war, the festival only lasted for one day, but it was extended to two days in 1963 and again to the present arrangement of three days from 1964 onwards. In 1965, when the festival was held for the second time in Chichester,

Leonard Bernstein's *Chichester Psalms,* commissioned especially for the occasion, were given their first performance at the final concert on the Saturday night. 'After the concert', recounts the *Prebendalian,* 'Mr. Bernstein came into the vestry, apologised for setting the words in Hebrew and congratulated us on the way in which we coped with them, and on the singing.'

Quite shortly before that festival Queen Elizabeth the Queen Mother had visited the cathedral. The school formed a Guard of Honour from the west door of the cathedral to West Street, and the Queen Mother stopped several times to exchange a brief word with boys and masters.

Under Mr. Birch the choir began to make regular appearances at the Chichester Festival Theatre. The first such occasion appears to have been in 1963 when they sang to H.R.H. Princess Margaret and Lord Snowdon, and as a reward were invited by Sir Laurence Olivier to the first night of Shaw's *St Joan.* This appearance was followed in December by the first Christmas Concert, at which the choir was accompanied by the Philomusica of London, and Fay Compton read some seasonal poetry and prose.

It was in this year also that Mr. Seal formed the first school choir, consisting entirely of non-choristers, to lead the School Services, for at this time it was customary for a Sung Eucharist to be held in the Lady Chapel three times a term.

Moving further afield, the cathedral choir had in April 1962 paid its first visit to Chichester's twin city of Chartres. Between concerts in the great Gothic cathedral the choristers, who were looked after by the Headmaster and Mrs. Bate, were based on the 'Maîtrise', a school for young theological students, and had their meals with local French families.

'Before the visit to Chartres', says Mr. Bate, who specialised in French, 'I taught the choristers about twenty French phrases, which I thought might be useful for them to employ in their contact with their French hosts. Two obvious phrases were: 'S'il vous plaît" and "où est le cabinet?", and another which I suggested they might use when they said "goodbye" was: "J'ai fait un bon séjour, madame".

'The Dean came to see the choristers off on their coach to the Channel port. He said, "Well, boys, the thing to remember when you go to France is that there is no need to speak French—just English, only louder!"

'The youngest chorister came to me on the boat coming back and said: "Sir, when I said 'goodbye' to my hostess, I said to her 'J'ai fait un bon séjour, Madame' and she was so pleased that she put both her arms around me and kissed me on both cheeks". Many years later I heard that this boy had got an Oxford degree in modern languages!'

Another quite new feature of life in the choir was the frequency of broadcasts, both 'live' and recorded, on radio and television. One such transmission occurred at Christmas 1961 when the choristers took part with choirs from various other countries in a Christmas Eve Carol Service on Euro-vision, but perhaps the most memorable programme was *Angel Voices*—a film about the life of choristers which was shown by the B.B.C. at Christmas in 1967.

Filmed for obvious reasons at an earlier time of year, the programme made a special feature of the boys staying on at the school after the end of term and included the inevitable pillow-fight, doubtless specified by the director as the most essential ingredient of life in any boarding school of this or any other period. The 'Christmas' dinner had to be cooked at a local hotel, but, when the director told the headmaster that he had arranged for the hotel chef to come in his white hat and carve the turkey, Mr. Bate quite rightly objected and succeeded in introducing a touch of realism by carving the bird himself.

The eleven years of Mr. Bate's headmastership were notable among other things for some interesting appointments to the staff.

In spite of his literary commitments, the novelist, John Harris, taught history for several terms; and two of the King's Singers, Alastair Hume and Anthony Holt, joined the staff in 1965 and 1963 respectively. The former left after two years to play the double-bass in the B.B.C. Northern Symphony Orchestra, where he shared a desk with Simon Carrington, also a Kingsman, and it seems probable that this was where the idea of forming a singing group of ex-King's Choral Scholars was conceived. Anthony Holt remained at the school for six years before deciding to make a career as a professional singer and he had not long been back in London before he was invited to become the baritone in the newly-formed King's Singers. Between school and university the writer and television reporter, Sheridan Morley, was also briefly on the staff.

Among the more experienced masters who joined the school in the 'sixties was Mr. R. H. Barff, known to friends and colleagues as Bim, who came from St Edward's School, Oxford, where he was a House Master and a Classics Master, to be Second Master at the Prebendal. Though after two years he was to return to his former stamping ground, he and Mrs. Barff eventually retired to Chichester and he was for several years a governor (lay adviser) of the school.

It is to this period in the school's history that the emergence of an esoteric organisation called the Crudgemen belongs. Its founder-members were all either former or existing pillars of the Prebendal staff, but at some later date others were invited to join so that the Society now includes two cathedral organists, a judge, a stockbroker, a public school headmaster, and two housemasters, as well as a few publishers, antique dealers and clergy, not to mention all the original King's Singers.

The word 'crudge' was originally applied to sacks of coal being carried to the cellar by way of the school dining-room at breakfast time, and 'crudging' came to mean the performance of any of the more menial tasks that fall to the lot of assistant masters. At the Prebendal School a master's duty day became his crudge day and the cry would frequently go up, 'Who's on crudge today?'

Mr. Ross states that meetings have been held all over the world, often in the most unlikely places, and that 'all that is needed is two Crudgemen and a bottle of Port or the national equivalent'. The society has but two aims, 'the first, to meet regularly and so keep in contact with each other; the second, to get the word CRUDGE into the *Oxford English Dictionary*.'

At Christmas 1968 Mr. Bate left the school to become Vicar of Lurgashall and, pending the arrival of his successor, Mr. Ross, who was already Second Master, was appointed Acting Headmaster for the Easter Term 1969.

Shortly before he moved, Mr. Bate made an important appointment in retaining Mr. Percy Woodcock, better known as Jim, as school caretaker and handyman. As Jim himself explains it, he was seconded by the Cathedral Works Organisation, for which he worked at the time, to do a spot of painting and decorating on the school premises. One thing led to another, as always happens at the Prebendal; Jim took a fancy to the place: and somehow or other he never returned to his original employers. This was to prove a highly advantageous piece of poaching. The world is entering the year 1984 and he is still there.

Chapter Eight

PERSONAL REMINISCENCES: 1969–82

THE HEADMASTER'S HOUSE, in which with my wife, Nony, and daughter, Marguerite, I took up residence in April 1969, was dignified in aspect, but awkwardly arranged. On the ground floor we had a large sitting-room, a small dining-room and an even smaller kitchenette; our bedroom, a tiny dressing-room and a private lavatory shared the first landing with the study at one end and the school office at the other; and the floor above offered a bathroom and a second bedroom cheek by jowl with another bathroom serving the cook and the under-matron who occupied the rooms in the attic. The two elements that were patently lacking were heating and privacy. The first was fairly easily supplied; the second we never attempted to achieve. Indeed, as year succeeded year, every room in the house except our own bedroom was at one time or another pressed into service to solve problems of accommodation arising in the school.

That this happened was largely the result of a deliberate policy of expansion, which raised the school population from 98 when we arrived to nearer 160 by 1978. Such an increase over so comparatively short a period was due almost entirely to an early decision to open the school to girls, and it inevitably entailed the reversal of the existing balance between day pupils and boarders.

When I first mooted the idea, I did so not only on the score that co-education was a healthy concept, but also because there was an obvious lack of independent schools for girls aged seven to thirteen within the immediate area of the city, and parents had begged me to consider the possibility of admitting younger sisters.

1. Effigy of Bishop Edward Story on the north side of the cathedral sanctuary. (Photograph: David Smith)

2. North frontage of the school on West Street, showing No. 53, No. 54 and the 13th-century schoolhouse.

3. The Cathedral choristers 1921-2.

. Choir practice in the Song School 1969. *L. to R.*: Clive Gregory, Simon Andrews, Ioward Blackett, Simon Darlow, Timothy Cawdron.

. Voice Trial 1969.

6.   The Cathedral Choir 1976. Choristers (*L. to R.*): G. Moore, P. Edwards, R. Civil,
R. Knowlton-Clark, A. Jones, N. Aiton, A. Wicks, K. Handley, P. Richardson, D. Newton

. Hirst, T. Dawes. Lay vicars (*L. to R.*): Mr. R. Cock, Mr. N. Chisholm, Mr. G. Knowles,
Mr. Robertson, Mr. M. Norris, Mr. M. Walsh, Mr. M. Pearce, Mr. J. Austin, Mr. N. Osborne.

7. Choristers returning from the cathedral 1969.

8. (*right*) The first three girls 1972. *L. to R.* Rebecca Powell, Lucy Phillips and Kate Farquhar-Thomson with Mr. and Mrs. Ollerenshaw.

9. (*below*) Opening of the new swimming pool 1972. Back row (*L. to R.*): The Ven. Archdeacon L. Mason, Mrs. Condon, Mr. Condon (Chairman of the P.T.A.), Mrs. Wilson, Mr. Ollerenshaw, Bishop Roger Wilson, Dean Walter Hussey, Mrs. Ollerenshaw. Front row (*L. to R.*): Paul Rowland, Simon Andrews, Ian Soutter, Julian Osborne, Faraj Saghri, Gavin Seabrook, Paul Condon, Christopher Powell.

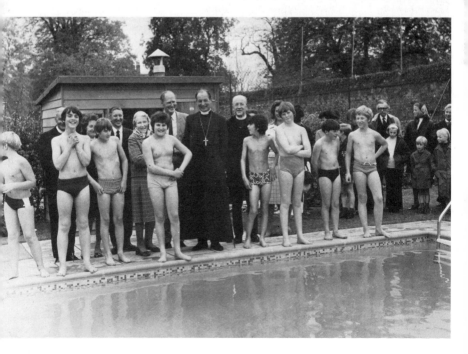

10.   The opening of the Richmond Building 1974. Front row (*L. to R.*):His Grace the Duke of Richmond and Gordon, Mr. Ollerenshaw, the Very Rev. Walter Hussey. Back row (*L. to R.*): Lady Todd, Mr. John McKerchar, Mrs. McKerchar.

11.   Boarders queueing at the hatch for tea 1977.

For a school that for centuries had catered solely for boys it was a revolutionary step to take, but the governors were remarkably open-minded and agreed to open the doors on an experimental basis to sisters of existing pupils on the understanding that the ratio of girls to boys should not exceed one third. The Dean qualified his acquiescence with the hope that it was not the thin end of an extremely large wedge. 'Girls', he observed, 'will only enter the Cathedral choir over my dead body.' The local press announced the change under the headline: 'Downfall of Male Bastion'. The staff shook their heads with obvious dismay. As for the boys, they publicly debated the motion that 'this House approves of co-education', the majority finding in favour, but their private utterances were more guarded and in some cases downright scathing. One fairly senior boy, who, to spare his blushes, shall remain nameless, was particularly outspoken on the issue. As chance would have it, he was sitting alone in the Selden Room when we ushered in Alexandra Bass, who was then about eleven and a prospective pupil. In a moment our homespun misogynist was on his feet, holding open the door, brushing his hair from his eyes and answering questions with an eager 'Yes, Miss Bass' or 'No, Miss Bass'. He was, like Saul on the road to Damascus, a total convert.

Initially parents were not unnaturally chary of placing their daughters in what was still essentially a boys' school; there was an understandable wish to see substantial numbers of girls before they committed themselves; so what was needed at the outset was a few pioneer spirits. We found them in Rebecca Powell, Lucy Phillips and Kate Farquhar-Thomson and their parents, who started the ball rolling in the autumn of 1972. Within five years there were forty-seven girls, and a few of them had even come in to board. Prebendal girls, in their dark blue cloaks with hoods lined in red, had become a familiar constituent of the West Street scene, and it was not long before their names began to appear alongside those of boys on the honours boards in the school dining-room, for it is a fact that they enriched the school with their industry and their talent. Indeed it was an earnest of things to come that at the age of only eight Rebecca Powell and Kate Farquhar-Thomson in their first term successfully carried the principal parts of Rosamund and Betty in the school's production of *Where the rainbow ends.*

Since the admission of girls coincided with a substantial increase in the number of boys applying for places, the governors in 1972 committed themselves to a major building programme. Already in November 1970, thanks to a generous legacy from the late Basil Shippam, himself an Old Prebendalian, a prefabricated classroom block bearing his name had been erected in the garden, and the following autumn, as the first stage of the planned expansion, a new playground was laid at the west end of the garden. This was to free the old school yard for the new teaching block and assembly hall, which were designed by Peter Fleming and officially opened by His Grace the Duke of Richmond and Gordon in September 1974. The Duke, unveiling a plaque in the Hall, reminded the school that his great-grandfather, 'who was born in 1819 and died in 1903—the year before I was born—was here in 1830 and so was his brother, Henry'. Shortly before the ceremony one of the children, who was clearly unfamiliar with the peerage, was overheard remarking to another: 'I know that the Duke of Richmond and Gordon will be opening the Hall, but who's Gordon?' To which his friend, equally unenlightened, was heard to reply: 'His dog, I think'.

To help the project, the governors had earlier launched an appeal, which brought a generous response from old pupils, parents and various philanthropic organisations and individuals, who reacted positively to the attractively illustrated appeal brochure with its text composed by Christopher Fry. The fund was further augmented by the proceeds of a special concert given by the King's Singers on behalf of the school. This took place at the Chichester Festival Theatre in the evening of 3 August 1975.

During the long months when the new building was under construction there were inevitable difficulties in circum-navigating its deep and extensive foundations (which revealed the remains of Tudor buildings and a number of bread ovens), and these were compounded by large-scale excavations in the precincts of the Cathedral, the foundations of which were also exposed as workmen reinforced them to arrest the process of subsidence. Access to the Palace Wing was preserved by lengths of wooden planking traversing the sea of mud, and some of the boarders, alarmed by the presence of human bones in the displaced earth, became convinced that the spirits of the dead would haunt the dormitories, where boys had traditionally made a point of scaring each other with tales of an imaginary grey lady, reputed to dwell on the spiral staircase of the medieval building. It was the school chaplain, the Rev. David B. Evans, who set minds at rest by paying a timely visit to the dormitories and blessing each in turn.

A growing school population called not only for new buildings, but also for additional staff. Over the years 1970-71 two new full-time posts and two additional part-time posts were created, while the teaching of French was enhanced by the engagement of a succession of young assistants from overseas. Among those that joined the part-time staff in 1972 was Mrs. Eve Powell (formerly Mrs. Salwey), who, after a gap of seventeen years, returned to help children with reading and writing problems, and the following year saw the appointment of Mr. David Smith, who as Head of the Mathematics Department and later as Second Master grasped and personified the intrinsic spirit of the Prebendal School. I personally owe much to him for his consistent support and good-humoured efficiency.

The scale of these major developments was such that they deserve pride of place in any account of this particular decade, but our first Christmas term—that of 1969—when these changes were still in the melting pot, witnessed at least one other innovation that was to have a lasting impact on the school.

Amid the joyful distractions occasioned by our daughter's whirlwind romance with the school chaplain, the Reverend Garth Turner (they were married in the Cathedral on 1 November), a meeting of parents and staff resulted in the formation of a Parent-Teacher Association. This led not only to improved communications between school and home, but also to joint fund-raising activities, which effectively transformed the amenities of the place.

Initially there were annual sponsored walks to West Wittering and back along a route carefully scouted out and charted by Mr. Ross. These marathons involved a complete day out in the early autumn; a mammoth picnic lunch was consumed on the shore; and those that undertook the return journey, who included some of the youngest in the school, could proudly claim to have covered twenty-two miles and show their blisters to prove it. In time, however, such strenuous exercises were replaced by jumble sales and summer fairs with themes that ranged from medieval through Continental and Roman to the wild west. On a purely social level there were also barbecues each summer under the trees in the school garden.

Within two years of the P.T.A.'s inception, the Purley pool, which was now past its prime and too small for the number of users, had been replaced at a cost of £3,600 by a professionally-dug swimming pool with a paved surround and its own heating and filtration plant. It was officially opened by the Bishop, Dr. Roger Wilson, in May 1972 and, as well as being used for class instruction and voluntary swimming in term time, was available for families and residents of the Close to enjoy during the long summer holidays.

In succeeding years the P.T.A. provided the school with, among other things, a hard tennis and netball court, athletics and science equipment, an overhead projector, a printing press and stage curtaining for the Hall.

The building was not often used for concerts as it was not as spacious as the Old Kitchen and it was acoustically inferior, but school plays, transferred to it from 1974 onwards, grew steadily more ambitious and showed an increasing tendency to incorporate music. This was no accident since a succession of gifted and versatile musicians came to occupy the rooms at the head of the palace staircase. Under Nicholas Cleobury, Ian Fox, Richard Cock and Jeremy Suter the school enjoyed a musical renaissance, and their interest in drama, harking back to the era of Richard Seal, made it possible to stage an all-treble version of *The Pirates of Penzance* (1978), musical transcriptions of *David Copperfield* (1979) and *Tom Sawyer* (1981) and two productions (1971 and 1977) of a home-made extravaganza entitled *Date Pie*, which, liberally inter-spersed with songs, purported to trace the history of England from Roman times to the present century. Particularly clear in my memory is the picture of Mr. Arnold Davidson, the Head of History and School Bursar, sitting, immaculate in dinner jacket, on the end of the grand piano and with the utmost solemnity lending his rich voice to the nonsensical narrative that linked the scenes.

For weeks before these shows Mr. Tilling, who was by turns School Sergeant, Secretary and groundsman, fashioned faithful replicas of antique weapons and armour, while Mr. Geoffrey Lea, who had joined the school as Science Master in 1968, burned the midnight oil erecting the stage and building props from dexion. These constructions were so heavy that it required the combined efforts of several strong men to change the sets, and I recall in particular a throne that lived in the staffroom between productions, a hollow tree that threatened to crush any who were rash enough to approach it, and a bed which, when the curtains opened for a dress rehearsal, proved to be already occupied by an exhausted Mr. Lea. Equally preoccupied during the run-up to every play was my wife, Nony, who designed, manufac-tured and fitted the children with an amazing variety of costumes and, when we left, bequeathed to the school a wardrobe of enviable range and durability.

The school play, involving, as it did, so many of the children and staff working shoulder to shoulder, was not only an object lesson in the value of teamwork, but also, by enabling the players to identify with stage characters, a wonderful dispeller of inhibitions. Apart from these obvious benefits, it was tremendous fun. I still smile when I think of a group of young masters happily dropping heavy objects from a great height into a bathtub full of water in order to simulate the sound of Israel Hands falling to his death in a tropical sea, and how, in connection with that same produc-tion of *Treasure Island* (1969), I must have surprised local people and perhaps even broken the law by driving through the city with a complete skeleton, borrowed from the hospital, in the passenger seat beside me. Then there was Mr. David Gutteridge (Senior English Master and Geography Master, 1976-83), who, like Alfred Hitchcock, always put in an unexpected appearance, appropriately costumed, on the last night of his own (and even other people's) productions.

Just as the plays made a fitting climax to the Christmas term, so did the concerts that occurred towards Easter. In fact, these proved so popular with parents and others that they were later supplemented by performances in the summer term of costumed oratorios, several of which were written and composed by Mr. Adrian Arnold (Classics Master, 1976-80), in conjunction with Richard Cock.

These activities entailed much practice on the part of the school orchestra, special choir and soloists, but so much enthusiasm had been generated by the music staff that the children were happy to give up their free time. The numbers of children learning one or more instruments expanded so rapidly that at one stage the orchestra comprised forty-five players, and in 1977 it was calculated that as many as three thousand individual music lessons were given in the course of the school year.

Not surprisingly, as the music flowered, there was a steady improvement in the harvest of examination results, and the numbers of boys and girls gaining Music awards frequently overhauled the academics, the combined total of scholarships reaching double figures in more than one year. We were especially delighted when non-choristers began to figure on the lists of music scholarship winners.

It would be wrong, however, to lose sight of the fact that it was the twelve choristers and the six probationers who were always at the heart of our music-making. Under the leadership of John Birch, whose reign of twenty-two years stretched from 1958 to 1980, they earned a high reputation, and people in quite distant places would speak with knowledge and respect of 'the Chichester sound'.

In 1976 the choir paid a further visit to France. On this occasion they not only performed in Chartres Cathedral, but also gave recitals in Paris, Versailles and Fontévraud. Their concert in the great abbey of Fontévraud had the distinction of being the first to be given there since the church, which had for over a century been part of a prison, had been restored as a place of worship and a cultural centre for the west of France.

Two years later they spent the greater part of a week at Kristiansand in Norway, where they took part in an International Festival of Church Music, and in 1979 they were back in France for ten days celebrating the Year of the Normandy Abbeys, singing Mass at Bec and Mont St Michel and giving recitals at Bayeux, La Lucerne, and St Pierre-sur-Dives.

As the choir widened their horizons, so, too, did the non-choristers, who from 1974 onwards were encouraged to join Long Expeditions that occurred in alternate years. In the early stages these reached no further than Rouen and Dieppe, where through the good offices of the Director of Education for Leicestershire (Mr. A. N. Fairbairn), the school was permitted to make use of the Centre Culturel Léo Lagrange for the duration of each visit. In subsequent years the Senior French Master, Mr. Stanley Prince, who was responsible for organising the expeditions, ventured further afield, taking parties to Paris and visiting Chartres and Versailles in their turn. By 1980 globetrotting had become so popular that the fallow years began to be filled with ski-ing parties, the first of which—in January 1981—was based on Fiesch in the Rhone Valley, the leading spirit being Mr. Arnold, who returned from Lancing College to take our beginners in hand.

There were no colours to be won for sports like ski-ing, but under the Guilds system, which I introduced in my first year, proficiency in this or any other extra-curricular activity could merit the award of a badge. These were produced in three colours and represented the successive stages—apprentice, journeyman, and master—to which medieval craftsmen had aspired. Recognition in three distinct fields at the Master level ensured for the boy or girl who achieved it a place on the Guilds board in the Hall and became an honour that was highly prized, especially by such as had no claim to academic distinction.

With Guilds as the spur, clubs and societies and fringe activities of all kinds proliferated, though inevitably much depended upon the skills and qualifications of the staff and their willingness to devote their time to the children. Among the most popular and long-lasting recreations stood carpentry (taught by Jim Woodcock) and table tennis, which in 1975 was moved to the Richmond Hall and thus allowed the old recreation room, already housing the model railway club, to be converted into a library, with a new door and outside staircase designed by Mr. Kenneth Sinclair. As staff came and went, other hobbies that flourished for varying lengths of time were sailing, dancing, riding, fencing, cookery, modelling, printing, drama, bridge, scrabble, chess, and campcraft, the latter owing much to Mr. Lea's summer camps on Arran or in the Lake District. Written and illustrated projects on every conceivable subject were also produced in pursuit of the coveted Guilds badges.

These pastimes were largely confined to the winter months, with the additional diversion (until the arrival of the video recorder) of fortnightly or three-weekly film shows in the library. The summer months took care of themselves with swimming, cricket practice in the nets, gardening, and camping, but never a year seemed to pass without producing a coterie of boys whose chief delight lay in noisy war games and running battles in the garden. Inspired by the television serial, the board game of 'Colditz' was much in vogue with them, and their excitement was intense when in the summer of 1975 the late Mr. Airey Neave, M.P., an old friend and the first Englishman to get away from Colditz, came down to Chichester specifically to talk to the boys about his experiences and his escape. This prompted a few enthusiasts to compose a letter to Mr. Oliver Philpot, who in 1977 obliged them by visiting the school and telling them about the famous Wooden Horse by which he effected his own escape from Stalag-Luft III.

One hopes that it was solely due to these illustrious examples that we had our own escapers' club. One small probationer in pyjamas and dressing-gown decamped rather than have his hair cut and was brought back to school after being found at the Fishbourne Road railway crossing, armed only with a Bible and an apple, and on another dark night a member of staff apprehended a chorister enveloped in a Ku-Klux-Klan-type of hooded gown who was heading for the playing-fields with the determination to foil an imagined plot on the part of wicked monks to land by helicopter and kidnap the Bishop.

Another inconvenience was the propensity of children to injure themselves by breaking limbs, which they always seemed to do in threes, taking care to include the captain of the 1st Cricket, Hockey or Soccer XI. This was matched by the tendency of the new fire alarm system to sound off whenever an apple turnover was left under the grill and sometimes with no provocation at all, but, in the light of what happened in August 1976, it was far better to be safe than sorry.

One Saturday evening two fires were started in the Cathedral during Evensong, and a third conflagration gutted the stair well in the east wing of the Bishop's Palace and damaged both the classrooms and the residential accommodation on the top floor. Fortunately, the building was unoccupied since the summer holidays had begun, but, when the school re-opened in September, several classes had to be transferred to Blackman House in Canon Lane, which happened to be untenanted at the time. A year later a man was charged with arson and was duly convicted.

By contrast with such sombre moments, if I were asked to isolate my most precious memories of the Prebendal School, I should be most strongly tempted to single out the weeks before Christmas. With the play over and the festive season approaching, the tempo of work inevitably slackened, so on the final Friday of the term I instituted a General Knowledge Quiz paper, consisting of a hundred questions, which all but the first-year forms attempted. Though the test provided a field day for resident clowns, it yielded enough hopefuls for the school to pick a team to compete in the Schools Challenge Contest. At the same time, of course, there was a rich harvest of unintentional humour, as when a spinet was identified as an unmarried woman and a maiden over as a married one. On the following Tuesday the boarders' term would end with a gargantuan feast by candlelight, for which everyone donned his most formal attire. Held initially in the dining-room, but later transferred to the Richmond Hall, House Suppers—as the occasion is called— originally ended with prefects' charades and sketches performed by the staff, but in our time these gave way to speeches from the Headmaster and the Head Boy, both of whom regularly sang or recited topical verses.

With the departure of the boarders, the twelve choristers, whose duties were far from done, would move all their goods and chattels into adjacent dormitories and embark upon a new routine of rehearsals alternating with spells of relaxation, parties and shopping expeditions in the city centre. In successive years one of the boys, who had clearly inherited business acumen, opened in Long Dormitory a soft-drinks counter that rejoiced in the name of Nutty's Bar and invariably netted a handsome profit for some charitable cause. Some time in Christmas week the boys would trim the tree in the Selden Room and set up a lighted crib in the senior dormitory, where in a moving little ceremony they would gather round with ourselves and the matrons and sing 'Silent Night'. Then the chaplain, the Reverend Bryan Marshall (Priest-Vicar and Chaplain, 1974–81) would say a prayer and bless the crib.

Traditionally on Christmas Eve, as the boys had to be up for the Midnight Mass, they retired to bed early and, once the lights had been extinguished, I would read or tell them ghost stories, which never seemed to prevent them sleeping afterwards. Problems were more likely to arise after the service when we tried our best to outlast them in order that Father Christmas (both of them) might go his rounds unseen. In the morning an appropriately-costumed Santa Claus distributed presents from the tree, and later in the day, following a visit from the Dean, who would bring a gift of money for each and every boy, there were riotous games on the private side of the building. 'Murder in the dark' was particularly popular as it presented the boys with the perfect opportunity to throttle the Master of the Choristers, but John Birch, it must be added, was a master of evasion!

Writing in the Cathedral Newsletter in 1976, I concluded an account of the school with the question, 'How do pupils regard the Prebendal School?' and continued, 'Judging by the number of old pupils (see note below) who return in after-years, the place exerts a considerable gravitational pull on its former inmates. They appreciate the family atmosphere; they remember with affection its architectural oddities; and one and all speak of it, without being able to put a finger on the exact reason why, as a happy place. Significantly, though they are not always aware of it at the time, the constant presence of the Cathedral in the background seems to exert a powerful influence, inducing a sense of security and an attitude of reverence that is good for a lifetime. I like to think that above all else that they learn here Prebendalians discover the truth of the school's motto: "Fons sapientiae verbum Dei".'

*   *   *   *   *

The Old Pupils' Association was for many years nurtured and kept alive through the efforts of Mr. Terence Banks, who as Secretary deserves their gratitude for his long service and organisational flair.

The Chichester Old Choristers' Association, founded by Mr. Richard Cock, is a more recent development and its annual meetings in July are attended by old choristers of virtually every age and vintage. This institution continues to thrive under Mr. Alan Thurlow, who succeeded Mr. Birch as Organist and Choirmaster in 1980, and Mr. Jeremy Suter, the Assistant Organist and Secretary of C.O.C.A.

APPENDIX I

Extracts from Statutes made for Chichester Cathedral by Bishop Ralph II, with the assent and consent of the dean and chapter, 26 October 1232.

Of the Office of Chancellor

The Chancellor by the ancient custom of the church must hear the lessons assigned for the right services in person, or by a fit person of competent experience, well learned in the method of pronunciation customary in the church. This he must do immediately after vespers. He can, however, if he wishes to lighten his labours, call the juniors of the second form and the boys of the third form and hear their lessons before that office. But whoever is going to read must present himself to be heard at a convenient time, otherwise if through mispronunciation or absurdity or otherwise he offend against the rule of the church, let him incur the penalty decreed below* against those who commit default in duties assigned to them by the daily table, which in the church are commonly called 'marances'.

*If a vicar, the loss of 1d. or 2d.; if not a vicar, chastisement by the precentor or his deputy; but if of the third form (i.e. a boy) let him be turned out of the choir or receive from his master or the precentor's deputy seven strokes, or, if he has committed a grave offence, fourteen.

Of the Boys of the Third Form

We decree also that ten fit boys be elected from the third form by the Schoolmaster and the Precentor's vicar and their names written in the Upper part of the Table near the margin* and when any one of them fails new ones are to be put in their place, and no one not in that number is to be entitled to any office in the inscription of the Table, unless he is one of the household or family of a canon.

*De pueris de tercia forma. Statuimus eciam ut per magistrum scholarum et vicarium cantoris decem pueri elegantur ydonei in tercia forma, et eorum nomine in superiore parte tabule juxta marginem scribantur.

APPENDIX II

Extracts from the ancient and approved customs of the cathedral which at a full chapter on the morrow of St Mary Magdalen, 23 July, 1247, were ordered to be reduced into writing and published.

Ancient Customs of Various Offices

The Dean presides over all the canons and vicars as to cure of souls and correction of morals.

The Singer *(Cantor or Precentor) ought to rule the choir as regards singing, and can raise or lower the chant, place readers and singers both for night and day in the table, admit the inferior clerks to the choir and, when orders are being conferred, read out the names of those admitted.

The Chancellor† ought to rule the school or present to it, to hear lessons and determine them; to keep, with the assistance of a faithful brother, the seal of the chapter, and compose letters or deeds.

*Cantor debet chorum regere quoad cantum, et potest extollere atque deprimere; lectores et cantores nocturnos in tabula notare, inferiores clericos in chorum introducare; in celebracione ordinum clericorum admissorum nomina recitare.

†Cancellarius debet scolas regere vel dare, lecciones auscultare et terminare, sigillum ecclesie, adhibito sibi fratre fideli, custodire, litteras et cartas componere.

APPENDIX III

Statutes of the School of Chichester made by Bishop
Edward Story, with the assent and consent of the dean and
chapter, 18 February 1497/8 and amended 23 January 1502
and 26 July 1550.

Preamble

Looking upon the no slight ignorance of the priests under
our charge, and the excessive predominance of wicked priests,
on account of the rarity of good Ministers of Christ in our
Diocese of Chichester appointed as they too often are without
sufficient piety, inasmuch as from causes of this kind very
many evils arise because as the sacred page bears witness in
the 6th of St Luke 'If the blind should lead the blind, they
both fall into the ditch', Wherefore the Text expressly says
in the 38th division 'Ignorantia' 'Ignorance the Mother of all
evils is especially to be avoided in God's Priests' And since
frequently serious evils arise from those under our charge
owing to wicked men and more especially if they are priests,
holding the office of teaching among the People of God as
the Text prophesies in the 4th of Leviticus where it says 'If
a Priest who has been anointed shall have sinned, he often
causes the people to go wrong' on this Gregory says—'When
a Shepherd goes through steep places the result is that the
flock follows to the precipice' for according to the sin of the
Priest have the people an opportunity to sin, thinking out
how to meet the above named evils since from the office
laid upon us we are bound to provide for the salvation of
those under our care as far as may be possible: at length we
thought that an increase of Grammatical knowledge would
be the best remedy against the above named ills. Not that
Grammar (which has flourished but little on these shores)
as Peronius bears witness is of avail for eternal salvation as
in the decree 'Li quis Grammaticam' in the 37th division
where the Text is at the end of the Grammars but *learning*
can ever avail to eternal life provided that it be employed to
the best uses.

THEREFORE for the foundation of a Grammar School in perpetuity in this City of Chichester, first calling on the name of Christ we have thought right to proceed in the following manner—In the name of God—Amen.

Mode of Appointment to Canonry and Prebendal Stall of Highley and Master of Grammar School

WE Edward by Divine permission Bishop of Chichester do decree, will and ordain for ourselves and our successors in perpetuity, with the full consent and assent of the Dean and Chapter of our Cathedral Church of Chichester and with the consent and assent of Master Nicolas Taverner, Canon and Prebendary of new Highley in our said Cathedral Church of Chichester, that with the first after this our Ordinance, and then as often as and whenever the Canonry and Prebendal Stall of Highley in our aforesaid Cathedral Church should have become vacant by death, resignation or from any other cause, that then the Dean (if he be present) but if not its president and Chapter or a majority of the same within thirty days, to be counted successively from the time of the vacancy becoming known, for us if the vacancy occurs in our time, and for our successors for the time being should to the said Canonry and Prebendal Stall of Highley aforesaid nominate one Priest well and sufficiently instructed in Grammar, and other Literature, and apt in teaching and expert in undertaking the office of teaching, on whom the said Canonry and Prebendal Stall of Highley without any undue delay with the duty, as is aforesaid of teaching in our Grammar School of Chichester according to our ordinance and Statutes as hereafter written shall be by us or our Successors conferred And if on the one so nominated as is aforesaid it should happen by us or our successors in any way that the said Canonry and Prebendal Stall are not conferred, then we will, ordain and decree that the aforesaid Dean and Chapter within thirty days to be computed successively from the time on which there should be perfect agreement concerning the impediment to the Admission of the one first nominated, should nominate for us and our successors, under the manner and form aforesaid, one other Priest well and duly instructed in Grammar and other Literature, and apt and expert in teaching on whom when appointed the Canonry and Prebendal Stall of Highley without any undue delay with the duty as is aforesaid, of teaching in our Grammar School, as pre-arranged, should be conferred, and if by us or our Successors or any one else except the one nominated by the Dean and Chapter as above noted, or if he be so nominated without the duty and care of teaching in our Grammar School in accordance with the force, form and effect of our ordinance and Statutes from this time made, given and delivered on him when appointed the Canonry and Prebendal Stall should be conferred, then we will, decree and ordain with the consent of our aforesaid Dean and Chapter that that appointment thus made should be of itself null, void, empty and of none effect, and that whatever act should from thence follow should be also 'ipso facto' null, void, fruitless and of none effect and we will, decree and ordain with the consent of the said Dean and Chapter, and consent and assent of Master Nicolas Taverner aforesaid, on our own behalf and that of our successors, that if we in our times or our successors for the time being in their time should have delayed thus to confer as aforesaid the said Canonry and Prebendal Stall of Highley, or any of our successors for the time being should have delayed to confer them beyond twenty days after he has been nominated by the above named Dean or his deputy and the Chapter as is aforesaid, provided that he shall have shown and presented himself to us or our successors for the time being, that then we shall pay by way of penalty and so shall each of our successors for the time being negligent in that respect, by way of penalty pay to the Dean and Chapter of our Cathedral Church of Chichester, for the time being, one hundred shillings of good and lawful English money to be used and employed on the fabric of our Cathedral Church of Chichester aforesaid, and not otherwise spent, and shall by such procrastination and delay to confer the said Canonry and Prebendal Stall of Highley beyond twenty days as is aforesaid, lose the power of conferring for that turn only, the same Canonry and Prebendal Stall of Highley aforesaid as often as we shall have been

negligent or our successors shall have been negligent by way
of penalty for negligence of such a kind, the power of
appointment for that turn only of the one so nominated
by the Dean and Chapter as above noted shall devolve upon
the Archbishop of Canterbury for the time being And if it
should happen that the said Dean and Chapter should make
or pay any charges, expenses, or pay any necessary sums of
money for nominating (as is aforesaid) inquiry or search,
then we will that after a nomination of this kind the one who
is appointed and admitted to the said Canonry and Prebendal
Stall of Highley should pay and refund to the same Dean and
Chapter the costs, expenses, and sums of money within a
month from the time when he thus admitted will then be
about to receive the fruits, and emoluments of the said
Canonry and Prebendal Stall of Highley.

NEXT we will, decree and ordain with the consent of the
said Dean and Chapter and consent and assent of Master
Nicholas Taverner, Canon and Prebendary of the New
Highley aforesaid that if it shall have happened that the said
Canon and Prebendary of Highley aforesaid whoever should
be the first after this and any other Prebendary of the same
Prebendal Stall for the time being should be taken ill or
otherwise rendered incapable of teaching or from any other
reasonable cause by permission of Master the Dean or his
deputy (which permission we by no means will should be
granted or given to him beyond thirty days in a year) shall
have happened to be absent that then in the meanwhile at his
own private cost and expense he shall find a deputy or
suitable substitute (which indeed we leave to the discretion
of the Dean or his deputy and Chapter or a majority of
the same) who shall instruct and inform well duly and free
of cost the 'Grammarians' and the other who come for the
sake of instruction to our Grammar School of Chichester
during the whole time of his sickness leave of absence or
impediment of such a kind and if he should have failed for
forty days to make this provision, then we will that the
same Canon and Prebend should pay by way of penalty to
the Dean and Chapter of our Cathedral Church of Chichester
or one deputed by them without any power of appeal forty

shillings of good and lawful English money, and if for a less time than 40 days he shall have ceased to teach and inform the boys and 'Grammarians' or not made any provision then we will that he should pay by way of penalty as is aforesaid, to the said Dean and Chapter a due proportion according to the time of the aforesaid sum of forty shillings and if for three months he should have ceased to teach we will then that the said Canonry and Prebendal Stall should in all justice be declared vacant. Thence when the Canon and Prebend becomes wholly and ipso facto extinct full power is assigned to our Dean and Chapter to nominate another.

NEXT we will, decree and ordain with the consent of the above named Dean and Chapter and consent and assent of Master Nicolas Taverner Canon and Prebend of New Highley above named as is aforesaid, that each Canon and Prebend of Highley aforesaid for the time being shall hereafter pay annually of the fruits of the aforesaid Prebendal Stall of Highley on the day of the anniversary to the aforenamed, Dean and Chapter or their deputy before nine o'clock of the same day for the future and in perpetuity under a double penalty, twenty six shillings and eight pence of good and lawful English money to be distributed among those present at our obsequies under a certain manner and form —to wit—To the Dean 20 pence, to each Residentiary Canon 12 pence, to the Prebendary of Highley 12 pence, to each Vicar of higher grade 8 pence, to each Priest Vicar of lower grade 6 pence, and to other seculars in their grade to each of them 4 pence, to the Subdean 8 pence, to the two officers of the Lord the King to each of them 8 pence, to the eight Choristers 8 pence, to the two incense bearers 4 pence, to the doorkeeper 4 pence, to the two sacristans 6 pence, to the 4 bell ringers 8 pence, and for burning wax round the tomb on the said day of the anniversary 2 shillings.

AND because the Dean and Chapter of our Cathedral Church of Chichester equally from the Statutes and Ordinances duly and lawfully before these made, delivered and duly published on this matter as from the dispensations and confirmations which have come from the sacred Apostolic seat and from the ancient and lawful prescribed custom which up to this present have come down, been enjoyed and used through the long preceding ages, have held and quietly and peacably received the fruits, returns, rents and emoluments all and individually of the said Canonry and Prebendal Stall of Highley aforesaid as often as and whenever they shall have been vacant through the death of the holder of the same for one whole year from the time of the death of the said holder, to be applied in and for certain uses as more fully appears from the ordinances made on that matter, therefore we will on our own behalf and that of our successors with the consent of our said Dean and Chapter and the consent and assent of Master Nicolas Taverner Canon and Prebend of Highley aforesaid after this for the time being should on the feast of S. Michael the Archangel or within twelve days next to and immediately following the said Feast should on each year in future and in perpetuity pay or cause to be paid to the said Dean and Chapter 31/8d of good and lawful English money, by way of indemnity in place of a vacancy of this kind arising from the death of the holder of this Canonry and Prebendal Stall of Highley and the said Dean and Chapter are not to receive and enjoy from henceforth the fruits, returns, rents and emoluments of that Canonry and Prebendal Stall from which 31/8d only is to be well and faithfully paid to the Dean and Chapter as is aforesaid. The same Canon and Prebend shall at the time of his admission find sufficient security for the said.

NEXT we will, decree and ordain with the consent of the aforesaid Dean and Chapter and consent and assent of the said Nicolas Taverner Canon and Prebend of Modern Highley aforesaid that each one of those who shall be hereafter Canons and Prebends of Highley aforesaid for the time day shall on each successive Friday in perpetuity except Good Friday and the Friday on which should occur the Feast of the Nativity, shall celebrate a requiem Mass for my soul, the souls of my father and mother and all our benefactors, and the souls of all faithful departed but on the other days on which he should celebrate except the day of our decease that he may celebrate Mass according as the Ordinal should appoint.

NEXT we will, decree and ordain with the consent of the said Dean and Chapter and the said Master Nicolas Taverner

Canon and Prebend of Modern Highley aforesaid that each
Canon and Prebend of Highley aforesaid who is hereafter
appointed by us or our successors at the time of his appointment and institution or by the Dean and Chapter at the time
of his Admission shall swear that under no pretence of his
Canonry and Prebendal Stall aforesaid or residence within
the City of Chichester or our Cathedral Church aforesaid
shall he claim any share at any time from the Common Fund
of our Cathdral Church of Chichester or receive any part
(excepting only when at all the obsequies and Masses for
the dead the King's Officers receive monies, when the above
named Prebends may receive monies, provided they are
present at the said obsequies and Masses and because we
have given certain vestments and ornaments to the honor of
God, the Blessed Mary and the rest of the Saints of the
Heavenly Court and for the use of the Canon and Prebend
of Highley aforesaid for the time being within the Chapel
situated on the Eastern side of our Cathedral Church of
Chichester aforesaid in perpetuity there to remain viz—four
vestments with their requisites—one red, one black, one
white, and the fourth and remaining one green, one chalice
wholly and fully gilt 13 oz in weight, two silver gilt cups
curiously wrought 5½oz weight and one Missal whose second
leaf begins 'mundi spiritus', also one pair of palls of green and
brown damask, and another pair of (Bardurus of Alexander)
with four broad clothes for the Altar and with the rest of
the belongings. Therefore we will and ordain that the Canon
and Prebend of Highley aforesaid at the time of his admission
shall receive the said vestments and ornaments by indenture
made between the aforesaid Dean and Chapter and the said
Canon and Prebend the one part always of the aforesaid
Indenture remaining in the hands of the said Dean and
Chapter, while the other part of the same remains in the
hands of the said Canon and Prebend:—and we will that
the said Canon and Prebend should well and duly treat and
keep all and all and each of the Canons and Prebendaries
of Highley aforesaid should in future and in perpetuity
treat and preserve them, and should the said vestments or
ornaments from any chance partly or wholly be diminished

or fail we will that the Canon and Prebend of Highley aforesaid for the time being should at his own personal cost and
expense in the place of those that are spoiled and destroyed
buy and procure new ones equally good and similar which we
leave to the opinion and discretion of the said Dean and
Chapter.

NEXT we will, decree and ordain with the consent of the
said Dean and Chapter and consent and assent of Master
Nicolas Taverner Canon and Prebend of Highley aforesaid
that each future Canon and Prebend of Highley aforesaid at
the time of his admission shall with his hand on the Sacred
vessels swear that he will well and inviolably observe our
ordinance and Statutes concerning and respecting the
Canonry and Prebendal Stall of Highley aforesaid and the
fruits of the same, and our Grammar School made and
founded, as far as he is concerned, and in like manner our
successors as Bishops of Chichester for the time being before
their installation shall swear on their own behalf themselves
or by their procurator duly deputed, and each of them shall
thus swear with his hand on the Sacred vessels.

NEXT we will, decree and ordain that in summer time in
future and in perpetuity the 'Grammatics' and others who
should happen to come to our Grammar School for the sake
of learning should on each ordinary day be within our
aforsaid Grammar School by five or very soon after but in
winter before six no reasonable cause preventing which we
leave entirely to the discretion and judgment of the said
Canon and Prebend for the time being or his deputy and
afterwards when the bell shall have rung for full morning
Mass to be celebrated within the Chapel of S. Gregory in our
Cathedral Church of Chichester we will that the said 'Grammatici' and other Scholars above named collectively and
individually should be present at the same morning Mass or
at least at the elevation of the Body of Christ in the same
Mass, and then peacefully and soberly should return to the
Grammar School above named and there when they shall
have re-entered the afore-named School immediately before
anything else shall the Canon and Prebend of Highley aforesaid begin or his deputy and with the Scholars in their turn

shall say the Psalm 'Deus Misereatur', with the 'Gloria' 'Kyrie Eleison' 'Pater Noster' 'Ave Maria' etc. the Scholars answering 'Deliver us from evil' 'Arise O Lord aid us' and with the Prayer 'O Lord, Holy Father, Almighty and Eternal God' and 'We bless the Lord' etc.—but on each evening before the departure of the Scholars from our said School after singing one antiphon concerning the B.V.M. and the Psalm 'De Profundis' being said by each side alternately—The Canon and Prebend of Highley if he be present but if not his deputy shall say 'Et ne nos' etc. finishing up with the prayer as long as we need human aid 'Rule we beseech Thee O Lord, Thy servant Edward' and when we shall have duly fulfilled our time with the Prayer 'Deus qui inter Apostolicos' our own name being always inserted.

MOREOVER we will that all and each of the Scholars of our Grammar School should in each year in future and in perpetuity at the obsequies of our Anniversary be present with sympathy at the time of the performance of the same obsequies being duly acquainted with it and there say two by two obsequies for our soul, the souls of our Father and Mother, and souls of all our benefactors and all faithful departed, while the rest say the Lord's Prayer, the Angels' Salutation and the De Profundis. But at the time of the celebration of our Mass we will that the Scholars say the commendations of Souls two by two in turn as is aforesaid. And the Mass over the Master of our School is to enter our Chapel, and there arranging the Scholars on each side of the same Chapel, and there to begin the Psalm 'De Profundis' saying that Psalm with the Scholars and should finish with the Prayers 'Deus qui inter apostolicos' and 'Deus fidelicium'.

NEXT we will, decree and ordain with the consent of the said Dean and Chapter and consent and assent of the above named Master Nicolas Taverner Canon and Prebend of New Highley aforesaid that each future Canon and Prebend of Highley aforesaid should on days, seasons and hours, suitable, convenient, customary and fit, diligently, sufficiently, well and learnedly, freely and for nothing teach, instruct, inform and chastise the 'Grammatici' and any others who come to our said School for the sake of learning, and never

under that pretext or any other from the same Scholars or
their parents or friends should receive any sums of money
or accept gifts or other presents except thanks given and
bestowed on him. And if he should neglect to teach as
before ordained, or should receive anything from the
Scholars or other persons above named contrary to this our
ordinance after two warnings a space of 20 days elapsing
between each of these warnings made by the Dean or in his
absence his deputy, we will that he should pay by way of
penalty to our Dean and Chapter of Chichester 10/- and
if when warned a third time he should contravene in any
way the above then we will that the Canon and Prebend of
Highley aforesaid for the time being should be deprived of
the said Canonry and Prebendal Stall of Highley aforesaid
and another be appointed in his place to the same as is
aforesaid, no reasonable cause hindering it.

NEXT we will, decree and ordain with the consent of the
said Dean and Chapter and consent and assent of Master
Nicolas Taverner Canon and Prebend of Highley aforesaid
that each future Canon and Prebend of Highley aforesaid
shall repair, keep up and sustain every kind of repair of
the houses, buildings, ditches and hedges of the same Prebendal Stall of Highley aforesaid and all and every kind of
repairs of the houses, buildings, chambers, walls and roofs
of our Grammar School, of Chichester well and duly placed,
at his own peculiar cost and expense, for his whole tenure
of office and should so give them up well and duly repaired
at the time of his death, and that the same Canon and
Prebend shall pay the tithes due to the Lord the King and
any other burdens whether they be more or less than those
named of whatever kind they may be belonging to the said
Canonry, Prebend Stall and our Grammar School, ordinary
or extraordinary in his time he shall pay, discharge and give
over, and that the said Canon and Prebend shall in no way let
out for hire or give at any future time in possession or grant
for nothing our Grammar School any Chambers or any part
of the same to Lay or Secular persons except the great
'Throne' [this is assumed to refer to the cellar] which we
grant to them provided that it shall be done without any

offence or inconvenience to the Scholars of our aforesaid Grammar School. Besides we will, ordain and decree with the consent of the said Dean and Chapter and the said Master Nicolas Taverner Canon and Prebend aforesaid, that the said Canonry and Prebendal Stall of Highley aforesaid after that for the first and next time they shall have become vacant from that time shall in perpetuity be unable to be held with any office by whatsoever name it may be reckoned, whether it be prebendal, rectorial, vicarial, chaplaincy to a hospital, free Chapel or any yearly office, whether the stipend be for any time long or short, and if the same Canon and Prebend of Highley aforesaid for the time being shall have gained or caused to be gained from the Apostolic seat or elsewhere any bull or authority contrary to these Statutes and Ordinances or in any way escaping them, or shall have accepted one gained in any way contrary then we will that the said Canonry and Prebendal Stall should be 'ipso facto' vacant and the said holder for thus acquiring or causing to be acquired or ratifying and accepting anything contrary as is aforesaid shall be wholly excluded and thoroughly removed from the same and every lawful title of the same which he had formerly required.

MOREOVER we give and grant to all and each of our successors in the See of Chichester in future and for their times all those tenements, buildings, lands, meadows, pastures and right of pasture with their belongings lying and situated in the town of Amberley, and places and fields of our Manor of Amberley aforesaid which tenements, lands, fields, meadows and pastures with their belongings we have bought and purchased with our monies lately from John Symond otherwise named Payes and William Symond otherwise named Payes brother of the same John late of Amberley aforesaid to have and to hold all the aforesaid tenements, buildings, lands, meadows, fields and pastures with their belongings in perpetuity to the same our Successors in the See of Chichester in future and for the time being under the following condition and no other viz: that if our said Successors or any one of them shall have failed to keep and observe in their strength and firmness well and inviolably our ordinance and Statutes about and concerning the Canonry and above named Prebendal Stall of Highley in our Grammar School above said as far as they are concerned collectively and individually or shall not individually and collectively have caused them to be kept and observed by others on their behalf, but shall have infringed, impugned, changed or acted contrary to them wholly or in part then we will that the Dean and Chapter of our Cathedral Church of Chichester may and shall 'ipso facto' from that time hold the said tenements, buildings, lands, meadows, pastures and pasture lands for alms purely and in perpetuity and may and shall rejoice in the same freely and quietly in perpetuity, our above named successors, each and all in perpetuity being 'ipso facto' wholly and entirely excluded from the same tenements, lands, meadows, fields and pastures and every share in the same.

BESIDES we will, ordain and decree that this our present ordinance for the future and perpetual recollection of the matter be written word for word on our Register Books, one copy of the same to be written in the form of a history and to remain in the hands of our Dean and Chapter while another is to remain in the hands of the Canon and Prebend of Highley aforesaid: and all and each aforesaid with the express consent and assent of the Dean and Chapter of our Cathedral Church of Chichester assembled in Chapter for this purpose in the Chapter House of our same Cathedral, and the consent and assent of Master Nicolas Taverner Canon and Prebend of Highley aforesaid we do ordain and decree and have ordained and decreed should be valid and last in perpetuity—to us only being reserved as long as we need it in human affairs the power and authority of changing, correcting, reforming, adding, taking away from, making to cease, rendering of none effect, or totally doing away with all and each of the aforesaid either wholly or in part.

FORM of Nomination of John Wykley B.A. to the above named Canonry and Prebendal Stall of Highley by the free resignation of Master Nicholas Taverner from the same being vacant after the above named ordinance To the Rev. Father in Christ and Master Edward by Divine Permission Lord

Bishop of Chichester Your Humble and devoted John Cloos LLD and DCL, Dean of the Cathedral Church of Chichester and Chapter of the same Cathedral safety and obedience in so far as they are due to the Reverend Father with honor, since before this it has been duly and lawfully established that as often as and whenever the Canonry and Prebendal Stall of Highley in your Cathedral Church of Chichester shall have been by any means vacant that then the Dean and Chapter of Chichester for the time being to you when the said Canonry and Prebendal Stall shall have become vacant in your times and for your successors in their times after the vacancy happening in any way whatsoever as is aforesaid may be able, have ability and ought to nominate one Priest to teach Grammar in your established Grammar School of Chichester suitable fit and expert so that on him so nominated as is aforesaid the said Canonry and Prebendal Stall of Highley should be conferred by you and your successors as is aforesaid in accordance with the force, form and effect of your Statutes and ordinances thence given and made. Therefore we the above named present Dean and Chapter do nominate to your Reverend Fatherhood at this present Master John Wykley B.A. to the said Canonry and Prebendal Stall of Highley aforesaid vacant by the resignation of Master Nicolas Taverner last Canon and Prebend of the same humbly praying your already tasted Fatherhood that on him thus nominated as is aforesaid may be conferred the Canonry and Prebendal Stall and you may cause and hasten the other things in accordance with the force, form and effect of the Statutes given and made in that respect, and that you may think it worthy to perform with favor the rest that belongs to your pastoral office. Given in our Chapter House of Chichester under our Common Seal on the fourth day of December in the year of our Lord One thousand four hundred and ninety seven.

In testimony and faith of all and each of which to this our present Ordinance twice written we have caused it to be strengthened and confirmed by affixing to it our own seal, and that if our Beloved Sons the Dean and Chapter of our Cathedral Church of Chichester and that of Master Nicolas

Taverner Canon and Prebend of Highley. And we the Dean and Chapter of the Cathedral Church of Chichester holding all and each above recited, and ordained and decreed by the said Reverend Father and our Master Edward by God's Grace Lord Bishop of Chichester do consent to the same and on our part do confirm and ratify and will to have the strength of perpetual firmness. In testimony of which thing we have caused our Common Seal to be affixed. And I the said Nicholas Taverner Canon and Prebend of the afore-named Canonry and Prebendal Stall of Highley aforesaid to all and each above done, performed, decreed, ordained and recited on my part do admit, approve and ratify and to the same do willingly afford my full consent equally with my assent that they may in perpetuity enjoy firmness—In faith and testimony of all which because my seal is known to few I have caused to be affixed the Seal of our Venerable Master Archdeacon of Chichester And we Gerard Borrell Arch-deacon of Chichester at the special and personal request and appeal of the above named Master Nicolas Taverner Canon and Prebend of Highley aforesaid made to us, in faith and testimony of the above named have affixed our Seal to these presents Given in the Chapter House of the Cathedral Church of Chichester as far as affixing the seals to them presents on the 18th day of February in the year of our Lord One thousand four hundred and ninety seven [more probably 1498] accord-ing to the course and calculation of the English Church.

TO ALL and each who will inspect, hear and see these presents Edward by Divine Permission Bishop of Chichester—Salvation through the Saviour of all and to apply undoubted faith, we bring and wish to be brought to the notice of you all and especially to those whose present or future interest lies in this direction through these presents that since in our ordinance to which are annexed these presents con-cerning our Grammar School in the City of Chichester there lately founded by us, we have reserved as long as in human affairs we need it the power and authority of chang-ing, correcting, reforming, adding, diminishing, interpreting, making to cease, making of none effect, and totally doing away with all and each contained and specified in the same ordinance, as clearly appears at the end of the same Ordinance. But because among the rest in our said Ordinance two clauses are inserted of which the first begins thus—'Next we will, decree and ordain' etc. in the twenty second line to be numbered from the beginning of our said Ordinance and extends to that clause 'And because the Dean' etc. and afterwards begins thus—'Besides we will, ordain and decree' etc. in the 58th line of our same Ordinance also to be counted from the beginning, and reaches as far as the clause beginning 'Moreover we give etc.' which clauses indeed as from the evidence and daily experience we have maturely and deliberately considered to be too strict and burdensome We therefore led by wiser counsel, still reserving to us as aforesaid the power and authority, do in perpetuity annul, make of none effect, and totally do away with, and wish to go for nothing the former of the two same clauses beginning thus—'Next we will', but the second or latter of the clauses of this nature beginning thus 'Besides we will', we change, correct and reform in perpetuity to last under the following form and manner—namely 'Besides we will, ordain and decree that the Canon and Prebend of Highley for the time being and his successors may lawfully receive, and canonically retain one Ecclesiastical Benefice only, Cure or otherwise together with the aforesaid Canonry and Prebendal Stall so that the aforenamed Canon and Prebend and Master of the aforesaid School for the time being may provide and have one suitable master (?) [Hosticarius] to teach under him in our aforesaid Grammar School for the relief and a share in the anxiety of the Master of the above named School and the use of the Scholars who come to the same School. In testimony of which thing and Testimony and faith of the change, correction, reformation moreover annulling, making of none effect and total annihilation of our aforesaid we have appended our Seal to these presents. Given in our Manor of Aldingbourne on the Twenty third day of the Month of January in the year of our Lord 1502 and Twenty fifth of our Translation.

TO ALL the Sons of our Sacred Mother the Church to whom these presents may have come George [Bishop George

Day] by Divine Permission through our most illustrious
Prince and Lord in Christ, our Lord Edward the Sixth by the
Grace of God King of England, France and Ireland, Defender
of the Faith, and Supreme Head on earth of our English and
Irish Church, everlasting Salvation in our Lord, be it known
unto you all that since Edward Story of good Memory once
Bishop of Chichester our predecessor moved with pious
intention has erected a Grammar School within the City of
Chichester and by its foundation among several acts and
statutes laid down, has determined willed and ordained
with the consent and assent of the Dean and Chapter of our
Cathedral Church aforesaid with the consent and assent
of one Nicolas Taverner the Canon and Prebend of Highley
in our aforesaid Cathedral that with the first after his ordinance as often as and whenever the Canonry and Prebendal
Stall of Highley aforesaid shall be vacated by death resignation or any other cause the Dean and Chapter if the Dean
be present, but if not his deputy, or a majority of the same
within 30 days to be counted from the time of such a
vacancy becoming known to the same Bishop in his lifetime
and after his death to his successors in the See for the time
being should nominate to the said Canonry and Prebendal
Stall of Highley aforesaid one upright Priest well and duly
instructed in Grammar and other Literature, moreover also
to undertake the duty of teaching Grammar on whom the
said Canonry and Prebendal Stall with the burden as is
aforesaid of teaching in our above named Grammar School
according to his Ordinance and Statutes written in that part
by the same Reverend Father or his Successors with any
delay may be conferred and the same Reverend Father has
besides willed that the aforesaid Priest nominated and
admitted to the aforesaid Canonry and Prebendal Stall not
only to teach Grammar in our School as is aforesaid but
also that he be bound to celebrate certain peculiar Masses
on certain days of the week within the Choir of the aforesaid
Cathedral as is evident by the above named Ordinance
annexed to these presents.

BUT we George the aforesaid Bishop on one part that a
discreet and learned and upright man may be appointed to

the said Prebendal Stall with the duty of teaching in the aforesaid School as has been pre-ordained from time to time to the Mastership of the Scholars who come there with the utmost zeal wishing and considering besides that this duty of teaching should sufficiently conveniently be able to belong not only to the Priests, but also to any other learned, wise, instructed and apt in teaching, and for that reason when as often as that the same Canonry and Prebendal Stall be vacant it might happen that a more suitable and worthy man may be elected to a duty of such a kind, and that the election may be made from a greater number, than if the election were made to the above from the order of the Priesthood only: and that the celebrations of Masses also as above specified in our Ordinance are not done and performed on these days as was wont—All and each of which aforesaid being duly pondered by us, moreover also mature and deliberate consideration being held in this matter with the Dean and Chapter of our Cathedral Church aforesaid with their express counsel consent and assent, moreover also with the consent and assent of Master Antony Clerke Canon and Prebendary of Highley we limit and interpret the Ordinance of the aforesaid Reverend Father and in our limitation and interpretation we do ordain, decree and will that (no Ordinance of such a kind being in any way a hindrance concerning the nomination and appointment of a Priest only to the aforesaid Canonry and Prebendal Stall of Highley with the duty of teaching in our aforesaid School) it shall be lawful and allowable for the aforesaid Dean and Chapter and their successors to nominate one Priest or any other upright man discreet, and learned, duly instructed in Grammar and apt in teaching and willing to teach to the above named Canonry and Prebendal Stall of Highley and our aforesaid School, as often as and whenever it shall in future have happened that the same be vacated by death, resignation, change, retirement, dismissal, privation or from any other cause—to us and our Successors to nominate and present by the ordinance of the aforenamed Reverend Father annexed to these presents with whatsoever of his Statutes Decrees and Limitations, as far as are allowed by the Laws and Statutes of our famous

Kingdom of England, in all other respects always to remain safe and in there strength. In testimony thereof we have caused our seal to be affixed to these presents. Given in our Palace of Chichester this 25th day of July A.D. 1550 the 8th year of our Consecration, 4th of the Reign of the above named King.

AND we the Dean and Chapter of our Cathedral Church of Chichester duly propped up in this matter by the King's Authority, all and each thro' the above named Reverend Father and Our Lord by Divine Permission Lord Bishop of Chichester holding firm to the above limitations, Ordinances and Statutes do consent to the same on our part and do moreover confirm ratify, and will to have the strength of perpetual firmness—in Testimony of which we have caused our Chapter seal to be affixed to these presents. And I Antony Clerke Canon and Prebend of the aforesaid Canonry and Prebendal Stall of Highley aforesaid holding to all and each of the above limitations, ordinances, Interpretations and Decrees as confirmed and pleasing do for my part admit and approve and ratify and to the same do willingly give my consent as well as my assent that they may keep perpetual firmness.

IN faith and testimony of all and each of which because my Seal is little authenticated and unknown to most therefore I have caused to be affixed to these presents the Seal of our Royal Majesty in Ecclesiastical Affairs on behalf our Archdeacon of Chichester.

GIVEN in our Chapter House of our Cathedral Church of Chichester as far as relates to the annexation of the seals to these presents 26th day of July 1550 A.D.

ON examination this copy agrees with the original in the hands of the Registrar or in the Registry of the Dean and Chapter of our Cathedral Church.

APPENDIX IV

Statutes of the Prebendal School of Chichester made by Bishop Richard Durnford, with the consent and assent of the Dean and Chapter, 15 March 1880.

WE Richard by Divine Permission Bishop of Chichester having after due examination reflection and consideration determined in the interests of religion learning and education to make certain alterations in and additions to the Statutes and regulations now governing the Prebendal School of our Cathedral Church of Chichester namely the Statutes commonly known and designated Bishop Story's Statutes dated in the year of Our Lord One thousand four hundred and ninety seven also further Statutes ordained by Bishop Story in A.D. 1502 also certain further Statutes dated A.D. 1550 also certain further ordinances or regulations issued by Bishop Carr in the year of Our Lord One thousand eight hundred and twenty eight Do hereby with the express consent and assent of the Dean and Chapter of our Cathedral Church of Chichester signified by their having caused their common seal to be affixed to these presents as well as with the full consent and assent of The Reverend Frederick George Bennett, B.C.L. Clerk in Holy Orders and Prebendary of Highleigh in our said Cathedral Church of Chichester signified by his subscribing his name and affixing his corporate or Prebendal Seal to these presents constitute and ordain the following Statutes as additional and amended Statutes for the Government and regulation of the Prebendal School of our said Cathedral Church of Chichester—

1. The Prebendal School shall consist of Two Divisions the Upper or Classical Division and the Lower or Modern Division. The Lower Division shall be constituted as soon as circumstances will permit. The whole to be conducted in the prebendal House and premises.
2. The Prebendary of Highleigh shall have the entire control and supervision of both Divisions including the power of appointment and dismissal of such Assistant Masters in both Divisions as may be requisite for the efficient working of the School.
3. The commencement of morning School in each Division shall be preceded by the reading of a portion of Holy Scripture and a short form of Prayer to be approved by the Dean and Chapter.

4. Religious instruction shall be given in both Divisions in accordance with the Doctrines of the Church of England as set forth in the Book of Common Prayer.

5. In the Upper Division instruction shall be given in the following subjects without extra fee, Latin, Greek, French, Mathematics, History, Writing, English, Grammar, and Composition, Arithmetic, Bookkeeping and Geography. Facilities are also to be afforded for instruction in other Modern Languages, Natural Science, Drawing and Music on payment of extra fees.

6. In the Lower Division instruction shall be given in the following subjects, English Reading, Writing, Arithmetic, English Grammar and Composition, French, Bookkeeping, Geography, General and Physical, History, Mathematics and Latin at the discretion of the Prebendary of Highleigh.

7. The holidays in any year shall not exceed thirteen Weeks except on the ground of illness certified by a duly qualified medical practitioner to be contagious or infectious without the permission of the Dean and Chapter and there shall be three School terms in each year.

8. The entrance fee of two pounds shall be paid on the Admission of a boy to the Upper Division and of ten shillings on the Admission of a boy to the Lower Division.

9. The School Fees for instruction in the Upper Division shall not exceed twenty four pounds per annum or eight pounds for each term and for instruction in the Lower Division shall not exceed nine pounds per annum or three pounds for each term which shall include all necessaries except Books. The Term fee shall be payable in advance.

10. All entrance and term fees and emoluments shall be paid to the Prebendary of Highleigh subject to his providing therefrom (1) fees for the payment of Examiners (2) money for the purchase of books for prizes (3) salaries for the Assistant Master or Masters.

11.   No boy shall be admitted to the Upper or Lower Division under the age of eight years and until he shall have passed a preliminary examination in reading, writing and Arithmetic to the satisfaction of the Prebendary of Highleigh.

12.   Boys boarding with the Prebendary of Highleigh or in any other house approved by the Dean and Chapter may be admitted as pupils in either Division.

13.   Boarding houses for Boys in either Division shall be licensed by the Dean and Chapter and subject to such regulations as the Dean and Chapter in conjunction with the Prebendary of Highleigh shall from time to time make.

14.   The Dean and Chapter shall be entitled to send any of the Choristers of the Cathedral to receive instruction in the Prebendal School on payment of the fees hereinbefore prescribed.

15.   The Dean and Chapter shall have power to nominate boys either in the Upper or Lower Division whether they shall or shall not have been admitted to the School (but subject to their passing the entrance examination if they shall not have been already admitted) who shall be styled Cathedral Scholars but such nominations shall not exceed in the aggregate one eighth of the number of boys in that Division at the time of any nomination. Such Cathedral Scholars shall have two thirds of the tuition fees remitted, shall be regarded as on the Foundation and shall not be dismissed from the School by the Prebendary of Highleigh without the opportunity of an Appeal to the Dean and Chapter—In case of a nomination to a Scholarship by the Dean and Chapter of a boy already in the School such nomination shall be made in concert with the Prebendary of Highleigh. When a Scholarship is vacant the Prebendary of Highleigh shall give early notice thereof to the Dean and Chapter.

16.   There shall be an examination once in every year of the boys in both Divisions conducted by an examiner or

examiners nominated by the Prebendary of Highleigh and approved by the Dean and Chapter. The examiners' report on the School shall be submitted by the Prebendary of Highleigh to the Dean and Chapter at their next meeting. Prizes shall be awarded to the boys for proficiency.

17. The Prebendary of Highleigh shall pay each Examiner a fee not exceeding ten pounds.

18. A book shall be kept by the Prebendary of Highleigh recording the particulars of Admission or departure of Boys in either Division the said Book to be produced at the Statutable Meetings of the Chapter in May and October.

19. The orders or regulations for the Prebendal School known as Bishop Carr's Statutes as also any directions contained in the Statutes of Bishop Story 1496 or in the additional amended Statutes of Bishop Story of 1502 or in the Statutes of 1550 are, so far as inconsistent with these Statutes, hereby repealed.

In Testimony whereof we have caused to be affixed our Episcopal Seal this twenth seventh day of February in the year of Our Lord One thousand eight hundred and eighty and in the tenth year of our Consecration.

And We the Dean and Chapter of the Cathedral Church of Chichester do hereby as far as in us lie consent and assent to and confirm and ratify the additional and amended Statutes hereinbefore set forth and ordained by the Right Reverend Father in God Richard by Divine Permission Lord Bishop of Chichester. In testimony whereof we have caused to be affixed our common and Chapter Seal this second day of March in the year of Our Lord One thousand eight hundred and eighty.

And I Frederick George Bennett Prebendary of the Prebend of Highleigh in the Cathedral Church of Chichester do hereby approve of ratify and confirm and give my consent and assent to the said Additional and amended Statutes in so far as I have power so to do to bind myself and my successors Prebendaries of the Prebend of Highleigh aforesaid. In witness whereof I have hereunto subscribed my name and affixed my Corporate or Prebendal seal this fifteenth day of March in the year of Our Lord One thousand eight hundred and eighty.

R. Cicestr.   John W. Burgon   F. G. Bennett
                            Dean   Prebendary

Signed sealed and delivered by the within named Richard Lord Bishop of Chichester in the presence of

R. G. Raper
Secretary to the Lord Bishop

Sealed with the Common and Chapter Seal of the within named Dean and Chapter of the Cathedral Church of Chichester, and delivered in the presence of

R. G. Raper, Chapter Clerk

Signed sealed and delivered by the within named Frederick George Bennett, Prebendary of the Prebend of Highleigh, in the presence of

R. G. Raper
Official to the said Prebendary

APPENDIX V

A list of those who had or may have had charge of the school whether as Chancellors or their deputies, Prebendaries of Highleigh or Headmasters, clerical and lay. In view of the uncertainty that surrounds the origin of the medieval foundation, names and dates relating to this period are in some cases conjectural.

1121	John	1554	Augustine Curteys, M.A.
1145	Peter	1556	Robert Oking, LL.D.
1148	Joseph	1561	Matthew Myeres, B.A.
1180	John d'Aquila	1570	Henry Blackstone
1192	Galfridus Aquillon	1571	John Penven, B.A.
1214	Hugh de Tournay	1572	John Beeching, M.A.
1222	Ralph de Neville	1578	George Buck, M.A.
1227	Eustace de Lereland	1582	John Sandford, M.A.
1229	Thomas de Lichfield	1582	Edward Bragg, M.A.
	John Clymping	1591	William Sale
1248	John de Arundel	1594	Hugh Barker, D.C.L.
1256	William de Bracklesham		M.A.
1280	William de Pagham	1604	George Elgar, LL.B.
1288 (?)	John de Lacy	1642	George Collins, M.A.
1330	Henry de Garland	1660	Thomas Barter, B.A.
1332	John Bishopstone	1665	John Baguley, M.A.
1362	Walter Bracklesham	1669	Francis Bacon, M.A.
1362	Henry Cokham	1685	Robert Tupp, M.A.
1367	Robert de Walton	1701	Thomas Baker, M.A.
1371	John de Kepston	1730	William Wade, M.A.
	Thomas Romsey	1768	Richard Tireman, M.A.
1386	John Shillingford	1776	John Atkinson, M.A.
1388	Lambert Threckyngham	1784	David Davis, D.D.
	Simon Russell	1797	John Stevens, M.A.
1396	Walter Meetford	1802	Moses Dodd, M.A.
1396	John Yernemouthe	1808	George Bliss, M.A.
1399	William Reed	1824	Charles Webber, M.A.
1407	Robert Neel	1840	Thomas Brown, M.A.
1430	John Stopydon	1879	Frederick G. Bennett,
	John Morton		B.C.L.
1439	John Fawkes	1912	William F. Pearce, M.A.
	Thomas Gyldesburgh	1931	Arthur S. Duncan-Jones,
1478	Edmund Lichfield		B.D.
1483	John Brackenburgh		
1496	Thomas Burwell	1935	Philip C. Manwaring,
			B.Sc.
1497	John Wykley, B.A.	1945	Philip E. Ellard-Hand-
1500	John Holt, B.A.		ley, M.A.
1502	William Hone, M.A.	1945	Andrew R. Duncan-
1504	Nicholas Bradbrigge, M.A.		Jones, M.A.
1521	John Goldyff	1951	Charles H. Sinclair,
1523	William Freynd, M.A.,		M.A.
	B.C.L.	1953	Guy F. Hepburn, M.A.
1531	John Tychenor, M.A.	1958	Bernard P. Bate, M.A.
1538	Anthony Clarke, B.D.	1969	Neville F. Ollerenshaw,
1550	Thomas Garbard, M.A.		M.A.
	(Lay Prebendary)	1982	Godfrey C. Hall, M.A.

INDEX

LIST OF SUBSCRIBERS

F. A. Aylward
Kevin Bailey
Terence Banks
Rev. Bernard P. Bate
Dr. & Mrs. E. W. Baxter
Anthony Beresford-Cooke
Jonathan & Avril Biggs
John Birch
Alexander Black
P. J. Blencowe
L. A. M. Boucher
Christopher & Helen Bradshaw
Louise Burrows
Dr. N. F. H. Butcher, M.A.
Nicolas Chisholm
Stewart D. Clarke
Nicholas Cledbury
Richard Cock
Mr. P. D. Combes
Mr. & Mrs. C. H. Curtis
Miss Winifred J. Curtis
Bruce G. M. Davidson
Mr. R. M. Davies
Jane Davis
S. F. Dayus
Henry Deane
Anthony Frederick Dobson
Harry Montague Dobson
Raymond George Dobson
Vick Dudman
R. B. Elliott
L. Evershed-Martin
M. R. Fairbrass
R. J. Fairbrass
Mrs. Heather Fisher
Dr. Keiran Flanagan
Mrs. J. Fordham
Olivia Gorman
The Rev. Canon R. T. Greenacre,
    Chancellor of Chichester
    Cathedral
Stephen Groves
A. M. & J. C. Gurney
David J. Gutteridge
Philip Fraser Hall
Lucy, Charlotte, Alice &
    Susanna Hammond
Roger Heath-Bullock
Guy F. Hepburn
Julia M. Hewitt
Raymond Hilsden

Anthony Holt
E. A. Horne
Mr. William J. W. Horton
Alastair Hume
Quentin John Hunt
Jeremy Hutchinson
Mrs. J. Jarrett
R. L. Jennings
Helen L. Kempson
Geoffrey A. Lea
John Lees
D. A. Lewis
K. Lippiett
Eileen E. Lock
J. S. McKerchar
Capt. & Mrs. P. McLaren
Alison Marshall
Revd. Bryan J. Marshall
Grp. Capt. L. Martin A.F.C.
    RAF (retd.)
Stephen William Need
Clive T. O'Donnell
Noel & Rachael Osborne
Dr. & Mrs. G. W. Owens
G. C. Papworth
The Rev. Canon G. H. Parks
    M.C., F.S.A.
Laurence Peterken
Andrew T. Porter
Stanley Prince
Paul Robinson
Keith Ross
David Ruffer
Fiona Scott
G. N. M. Scoular
Richard Seal
John Martin Selsby
Dave Smith
Nicholas O. M. R. Snowden
Alan Thurlow
Robert Toomer
Noel G. J. Tuck
David W. Vincent
Andrew & Alisdair Webb
Neil Weston
Adam Whittle
Mrs. R. A. Williams
J. C. Wood-Roe
K. H. Wright
James, Sarah & Adam Youatt